CONTENTS

ABOUT THIS BOOK

This *Step by Step Guide* has been produced by the editors of Insight Guides, whose books have set the standard for visual travel guides since 1970. With top-quality photography and authoritative recommendations, this guidebook brings you the best of Egypt's Nile region in a series of 14 tailor-made tours.

WALKS AND TOURS

The tours in the book provide something to suit all budgets, tastes and trip lengths. As well as covering the Nile's classic attractions, the routes include lesser-known sights. The tours embrace a range of interests, so whether you are a fan of museums, a gourmet, a lover of nature or have kids to entertain, you will find an option to suit.

We recommend that you read the whole of a tour before setting out. This should help you to familiarise yourself with the route and enable you to plan where to stop for refreshments – options for this are shown in the 'Food and Drink' boxes, recognisable by the knife-and-fork sign, on most pages.

Above: highlights of the Nile: the extraordinary pyramids; traditional felucca sailing boat on the Nile; the Temple of Horus at Edfu; the rooftops of Cairo; the vast Temple of Rameses II at Abu Simbel.

For our pick of the tours by theme, consult Recommended Tours For... *(see p.6–7)*.

OVERVIEW

The tours are set in context by this introductory section, giving an overview of the Nile region to set the scene, plus background information on food and drink, shopping, Ancient Egypt's religion and architecture, and entertainment. A succinct history timeline highlights the key events that have shaped Egypt's history over the centuries.

DIRECTORY

Also supporting the tours is a Directory chapter, comprising a user-friendly A–Z of practical information, our pick of where to stay while you are visiting the Nile region and select restaurant listings; these eateries complement the more low-key cafés and restaurants that feature within the tours and are intended to offer a wider choice for evening dining. Also included here are nightlife listings and, on p.124, a short but handy glossary.

The Author

Frances Linzee Gordon's fervour for travel was first sparked by a school scholarship to Venice aged 17. Since then she's travelled in over 100 countries, including most of those in the Middle East, for which she has a special passion. She holds an MA in Asian (Middle Eastern) and African Studies from London's SOAS, where she is also studying Arabic. Frances writes travel books, features for newspapers and magazines, and also presents and consults for TV and radio. She also lectures on countries and travel, taking every opportunity to encourage women to travel, believing that her gender is a help, not a hindrance, when negotiating the hurdles of the road.

Some of the tours in this book were originally conceived by Sylvie Franquet.

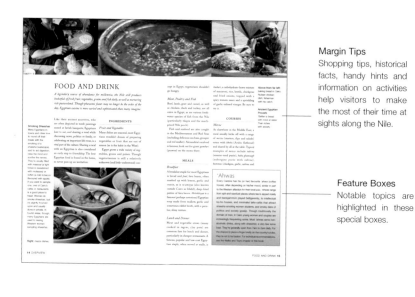

Margin Tips

Shopping tips, historical facts, handy hints and information on activities help visitors to make the most of their time at sights along the Nile.

Feature Boxes

Notable topics are highlighted in these special boxes.

Key Facts Box

This box gives details of the approximate distance covered on the tour, plus an estimate of how long it should take. It also states where the route starts and finishes, and gives key travel information such as which days are best to do the route or handy transport tips.

Footers

Look here for the tour name, a map reference and the main attraction on the double-page.

Food and Drink

Recommendations of where to stop for refreshment are given in these boxes. The numbers prior to each restaurant/café name link to references in the main text. Restaurants in the Food and Drink boxes are plotted on the maps, where coverage allows.

The £ signs at the end of each entry (except for those that only serve drinks) reflect the approximate cost of a two-course meal for one, with a glass of house wine. These should be seen as a guide only. Price ranges, also quoted on the inside back flap for easy reference, are:

££££	over £50
£££	£25–50
££	£5–25
£	under £5

Route Map

Detailed cartography shows the tour clearly plotted with numbered dots. For more detailed mapping, see the pull-out map slotted inside the back cover.

ADVENTURE-SEEKERS

Trek through burning desert or hire a camel to visit St Simeon's Monastery (tour 10), sail a felucca to Saheylle Island navigating the First Cataract (tour 11) or gallop a horse at sunset amid the pyramids (tour 2).

RECOMMENDED TOURS FOR...

ARCHITECTURE AFICIONADOS

Span 3,500 years of architecture, starting with pharaonic pyramids and temples (tours 2, 7 and 8), then Roman-era edifices (tours 5, 6, 9 and 11), medieval monuments (tours 3 and 4) and a 21st-century library (tour 6).

BOAT JUNKIES

Absorb the Nile to the full on a four-day cruise of Lake Nasser (tour 14), visit Aswan's Islands on a felucca (tours 10 and 11) and ride on a ferry to Luxor's West Bank (tour 8).

CAFÉ ADDICTS

Explore Alexandria's atmospheric Old-World cafés (tour 6), seek out Cairo's iconic coffee houses deep in Khan Al Khalili Bazaar (tours 1 and 3) or take tea near the Egyptian Museum (tour 1).

FOOD FIENDS

Tuck into a plate of Alexandrian prawns (tour 6) or a Nile perch (tour 14); sample *koshari*, Egypt's carb-packed national dish (tour 3) or *ta'amiyya* (felafel; tour 1), then try a refreshing *karkadeh* (hibiscus juice) served hot or cold or *asab* (sugarcane juice; tour 13).

INSIGHT GUIDES

THE NILE
Step by Step

APA PUBLICATIONS   L
Part of the Langenscheidt Publishing Group

MUSEUM FANATICS

Both Cairo (for Egyptian antiquities, tour 1; textiles, tour 3; oriental arts and crafts, tour 4; and Coptic artefacts, tour 5) and Alexandria (Greco-Roman, jewellery and historical artefacts, tour 6) have enough choice to satisfy the most ardent museum fan.

PHARAOH-HUNTERS

Egypt's great pharaohs left behind some of the greatest monuments and treasures ever created. Track them down on tours including those of Cairo (tour 1), Giza (tour 2), Luxor (tours 7 and 8) and Aswan (tour 12).

SHOW-SEEKERS

Don't miss Egypt's famous belly dancers, erstwhile entertainers of the pharaohs (tour 2), the spinning Sufis (tour 3), the theatrical Sound and Light shows (tours 7 and 13) or just stargaze Lake Nasser's skies (tour 14).

SOUQ-AHOLICS

No Middle Eastern trip is complete without a bit of haggling in the souqs. Pit your skills against Cairo's wily vendors at Khan Al Khalili (tours 1 and 3) or in Aswan's ancient souq (tour 10).

VISITORS TO TEMPLES, CHURCHES, MOSQUES AND SYNAGOGUES

A major centre for at least four religions, Egypt boasts temples to pharaonic gods (tours 7, 8, 11, 12 and 13), beautiful Coptic churches (tour 5), exquisite mosques (tours 3 and 4) and even a synagogue (tour 5).

OVERVIEW

An overview of the geography, customs and culture of the Nile in Egypt, plus illuminating background information on food and drink, shopping, entertainment, architecture and history.

INTRODUCTION

The Nile, the longest river in the world, has also nurtured its greatest civilisation. Ancient Egypt's monuments have struck visitors dumb for millennia. Today's Egypt also offers excellent value for money, a well-developed tourism infrastructure, diverse activities and a unique Egyptian eagerness to please that is rarely found elsewhere.

Beyond the Nile
Bar the narrow lining of fertile and irrigated soil each side of the Nile, desert covers most of Egypt. East of the Nile Valley stretches the Eastern Desert (also known as the Arabian Desert) bordered by the Red Sea Mountains. West of the Nile Valley lies the vast Western Desert (or Libyan Desert), part of Africa's great Sahara, the largest desert on earth. Sand occupies a huge 93 percent of Egypt's landmass.

Egypt owes its existence, history and culture to the Nile. Since pharaonic times, Egyptians have attempted to harness the powers of the Nile (most recently Gamal Abd An Nasser's infamous High Dam, *see p.85*), graphically demonstrating the country's continuing dependence on its river. If you fly into Luxor, Aswan or Abu Simbel, from the plane you will see Egypt for what it is: the thinnest green line enclosed on the east and west by infinities of sand.

Along this line, there grew up and flourished for over 3,000 years (until the Roman period) a mighty kingdom and series of wealthy dynasties. Preserved by the country's hot, dry climate and often buried by the sands, Ancient Egypt's life and culture have survived. It constitutes one of the oldest, best-preserved and richest civilisations the world has ever known.

Though some visitors find today's Egypt hard to reconcile with past glories – poverty is pervasive, unemployment rampant, and inflation, corruption and national debt among the many malaises afflicting the country, Egypt's spirit of resilience survives, as does her humour in hardship and innate sense of entrepreneurship. Tourism is still the country's most important industry. It – like everything else – revolves around the Nile.

LAYOUT

Like the course of the country's river – and its chronology – the book begins with Old Kingdom Cairo, where most visitors arrive, then leads southwards, taking in all the Nile's major monuments, including New Kingdom Luxor and the post-pharaonic temples between Luxor and Aswan.

Tours are also suggested to Alexandria northwest of Cairo beyond the Nile's delta, and to Abu Simbel in the far south, via the recently created Lake Nasser along with its little-visited but well-worthwhile Nubian temples. The tours can also be done in reverse order or cherry-picked – each is designed to work alone.

Welcoming tourists for several hundred years, Egypt has had time to build up one of the best tourism infrastruc-

tures in the world, with a good range and standard of hotels and restaurants, as well as decent transport links between towns and sites.

GEOGRAPHY

Egypt's great river defines her geography. Bisecting the country, the Nile flows due north from Sudan through Egypt all the way to the Mediterranean Sea. The Nile has two major tributaries, the Blue Nile, a product of the Ethiopian Highlands, and the White Nile, which begins at Lake Victoria in Uganda. They meet at the Sudanese capital of Khartoum, then continue northwards to the Mediterranean.

Just north of Cairo, the Nile branches into multiple tributaries, forming the 200km (124-mile) wide delta, home to some of the most intensively farmed land in the world.

CLIMATE

As a rule of thumb, Egypt has a desert climate: hot and dry. The further south you get, the hotter temperatures become. In Aswan and Abu Simbel, they can exceed 50°C (122°F) in summer.

In Cairo and the north, the winter months (December to February) as well as the spring and winter nights can seem cool (dropping to around 10°C/50°F or less). Skies can also be overcast in Cairo.

Bar Alexandria and the Mediterranean coast, most of Egypt receives negligible rainfall (Aswan receives an average of about 2mm a year), and during March and April, the famous *khamsin* (a dry, hot and dusty North African wind) blows.

When to Go

The best time to visit is during the spring (March to May) or autumn (October to November).

December to February boast perfect temperatures for southern Egypt (including Abu Simbel, Aswan and Luxor), but this is also the peak season for hotels, cruise ships and so on.

Above from far left: woman in Cairo's alabaster-faced Mosque of Muhammad Ali *(see p.55)*; banks of the Nile, Lake Nasser; statue of the God Ptah.

Below: camels at market.

Above: Luxor, floodlit by night; young women in Cairo Bazaar.

Early Souvenirs
Early travellers marked their trips by incising their names in often large, neatly carved letters on the monuments. They also liked to return with 'authentic' souvenirs. Less expensive than the antiques and treasures touted at the sites and hotels were mummies. Travellers bought them whole or in parts (easier to pack in the suitcase), and diaries recount early cruise passengers flinging mummies from boats when they began to get a little gamey.

June to August is the low season except on the coast, where southern Europeans and Gulf Arabs collect.

HISTORY

The Nile Valley is the birthplace of one of the oldest and greatest civilisations the world has ever known. For nearly 3,000 uninterrupted years, Egypt's kings and pharaohs ruled over a highly organised, cultured and sophisticated state, when most of Europe was still living in caves and hunting with clubs. To Ancient Egypt, also, the world owes major advances in the sciences and arts. Its influence can still be felt in our political, religious and social systems today. Increasingly, modern scholarship is viewing Ancient Egyptian society as a much more equitable, democratic and community-conscious society than was previously thought *(for key dates in history, see p.32–3).*

POLITICS

Belonging to the original gang of 'Free Officers' (who fought for independence from the British, and deposed King Farouk in 1952), Hosni Mubarak is certainly showing his age. Head of the ruling National Democratic Party (NDP), he is also head of the state and the armed forces. He additionally appoints all government ministers, and has the power to dissolve the People's Assembly practically at will.

In response to pressure both at home and abroad, Mubarak has gradually introduced greater democracy, with general elections for the People's Assembly held for the first time in 2005, and with a wider range of political parties being allowed to operate.

The Muslim Brotherhood is now the leading opposition party in Egypt, winning a quarter of seats in Parliament in 2005. However, Mubarak has cracked down heavily on the Islamist movements that threaten both his regime and any foreign influences that are seen as corrupting, including tourism. Since 1993, Amnesty International has consistently reported serious human-rights abuses and political violence, including mass arrests and torture.

The big question currently on everyone's lips in Egypt and abroad is who will succeed Mubarak. The latter, increasingly showing signs of ill health, clearly favours his son, Gamal; the rest of the country is less sure.

ECONOMICS

Egypt's main economic challenge is to cope with its exploding population. Agricultural land is limited, and at least half of the country's food is currently imported.

Other economic problems include a weak Egyptian pound, severe housing shortages, low literacy levels, infrastructure underinvestment, and a heavily bureaucratic, inefficient and

slow administration (a third of the workforce find employment here and in the defence forces).

POPULATION

Egypt's population – now not far off 80 million – is booming, increasing by around a million every 10 months. Egypt's Nile Valley itself threatens to become one continuous settlement. Cairo, home to at least 20 million, qualifies as one of the largest cities in the world and one of its most densely populated. The fertile Nile Valley is inhabited by 92 percent of Egypt's population. Many work as farmers practising a form of agriculture that has changed surprisingly little since the time of the pharaohs, planting some of the same crops and using some of the same (or similar) tools and techniques.

The People

Though Egyptians love to boast pharaonic parentage, a few centuries and conquerors, including Persian, Greek, Roman, Arab and Ottoman peoples, have diluted it. The typical Egyptian is religious but also loves life's pleasures. He/she marries young and has at least three children (the wife stays at home), a strong sense of pride, of family and of community values, and a healthy sense of humour.

In general, people in the south of the country, and the countryside, tend to be more conservative (epitomised by the women clad in all-black *abeyyas*/robes and *burkhas*/masks) than their northern counterparts, particularly in Cairo.

Indigenous Peoples

Inhabiting the Western and Eastern Deserts and the Sinai are Egypt's Bedouin, whose diminishing numbers are estimated at around half a million. Even fewer in numbers and still more threatened are the Egyptian Berbers who inhabit the area around the Siwa Oasis and Western Desert. The Berbers boast their own language (unrelated to Arabic) and distinct culture.

More likely to be encountered by travellers to the Nile are the Nubian people who have inhabited the southern Nile Valley (from Aswan to Sudan) since ancient times. Easily distinguishable for their darker skin and more Central African features, they regrettably lost much of their land (and culture) to Lake Nasser when the High Dam was built (*see also p.82 and p.85*).

Above from far left: monumental pharaonic head, Abu Simbel; Islamic-style building in Cairo; fishermen on the Nile.

Baksheesh
In a country where many salaries are insufficient to live on and where no social support system exists, many Egyptians depend on the earning of 'extras' to survive. And it's not just tourists who are targeted. Egyptian themselves pay such gratuities – called baksheesh – for the smallest services and see it as a part of daily life. Usually just an Egyptian pound or two suffice; more is expected in the larger hotels or touristy areas. It's a good idea to visit a bank soon after arrival and break large notes into smaller notes and coins so that you have a ready supply at hand. It may be an irritation and a nuisance, but for many Egyptians it's a lifeline.

Left: Luxor temple at night.

FOOD AND DRINK

A legendary source of abundance for millennia, the Nile still produces basketfuls of fresh fruit, vegetables, grains and fish daily, as well as nurturing rich pastureland. Though pharaonic feasts may no longer be the order of the day, Egyptian cuisine is more varied and sophisticated than many imagine.

Like their ancient ancestors, who are often depicted in tomb paintings seated at lavish banquets, Egyptians love to eat, and sharing a meal while discussing news, politics or family, or celebrating an important life event, is a vital part of the culture. Sharing a meal with an Egyptian is also considered an early step to friendship. The best Egyptian food is found in the home, so never pass up an invitation.

INGREDIENTS

Fruit and Vegetables

Many dishes are seasonal; most Egyptians wouldn't dream of preparing vegetables or fruit that are out of season (as is the habit in the West).

Egypt grows a wide variety of vegetables, grains and pulses. Though vegetarianism is still a relatively unknown (and little-understood) con-

Smoking *Sheeshas*
Many Egyptians in towns and cities love to round off their meals with the smoking of a *sheesha* (waterpipe), said to aid digestion, relax the mind and soothe the nerves. They're usually filled with *maassal* (a light tobacco sweetened with molasses) or *tuffah* (a mild tobacco flavoured with apple). One of Cairo's cafés or restaurants is a good place to head to sample one. Women do smoke *sheeshas*, but it's slightly frowned upon and usually done in private. In tourist areas, though, many Egyptians are used to seeing Western women sampling *sheeshas*.

Right: *mezze* dishes.

cept in Egypt, vegetarians shouldn't go hungry.

Meat, Poultry and Fish

Beef, lamb, goat and camel, as well as chicken, duck and turkey, are all eaten in Egypt, as are various freshwater species of fish from the Nile (particularly tilapia and the much-prized Nile perch).

Fish and seafood are also caught in the Mediterranean and Red seas (including delicious sea bass, grouper and red mullet). Alexandria's seafood is renowned; look out for giant *gambari* (prawns) on the menu there.

MEALS

Breakfast

A breakfast staple for most Egyptians is bread and *fuul*, fava beans, often mashed up with lemon, garlic and cumin, as is *ta'amiyya* (also known outside Cairo as felafel), deep-fried patties of fava beans. *Molokhiyya* is a famous (perhaps notorious) Egyptian soup made from mallow, garlic and sometimes rabbit broth, with a peculiar, slimy texture.

Lunch and Dinner

Meat and vegetable stews (many cooked in *tagens*, clay pots) are common fare for lunch and dinner, particularly in cheaper restaurants. A popular and low-cost Egyptian staple, often served at stalls, is *koshari*, a carbohydrate-heavy mixture of macaroni, rice, lentils, chickpeas and fried onions, topped with a spicy tomato sauce and a sprinkling of garlic-infused vinegar. Be sure to try it while you're in Egypt.

COURSES

Mezze

As elsewhere in the Middle East, a meal usually kicks off with a range of *mezze* (starters, dips and salads), eaten with *khobz* (Arabic flatbread) and shared by all at the table. Typical examples of *mezze* include *tahina* (sesame-seed purée), *baba ghanough* (aubergine purée with *tahina*), *hummus* (chickpea, garlic, *tahina* and

'Ahwas

Every Cairene has his (or her) favourite 'ahwa (coffee house), often depending on his/her mood, similar in part to the Western affection for their local pub. 'Ahwas range from spit-and-sawdust places, where tea is sipped noisily and backgammon played belligerently, to intellectual bo-ho houses, and minimalist latte-cafés that attract sheesha-smoking women students, and smoky dens of politics and society gossip. Though traditionally the domain of men, in Cairo young women and couples are increasingly frequenting some. Most 'ahwas serve non-alcoholic drinks, along with sheeshas; a very few serve beer. They're generally open from 7am to 2am daily. For the chance to place a finger briefly on the country's pulse, they're not to be beaten. For individual recommendations, see the Walks and Tours chapter of this book.

The Pharaoh's Kitchen
Co-written by Magda Mehdawy (author of the popular *My Egyptian Grandmother's Kitchen*), this new book contains nearly 100 recipes drawn from Ancient Egypt. Beautifully illustrated with colourful scenes from tombs and temples, as well as museum objects and artefacts, the book gives insights into ancient food cultivation, preparation and presentation, as well as culinary equipment, etiquette and methods. It's published by the AUC (American University in Cairo Press; *see p.38*).

lemon purée), *torshi* (pickled vegetables), *salata baladi* (literally; 'my country's salad' – tomato, cucumber and lettuce finely chopped with cumin and lime), *gargeer* (local rocket salad), *wara ainab* (stuffed vine leaves) and *kibbah* (fried ball of cracked wheat stuffed with ground beef).

Mains

Main courses very often comprise grilled meat such as *shish kebab* (lamb or beef on skewers), *kofta* (minced meat on skewers), *shish taouk* (skewer of chicken marinated in lemon and garlic) or *firekh* (roast chicken). *Hamam* (pigeon) is considered a delicacy and is either grilled or stuffed with *fireek* (green wheat) or fenugreek.

Desserts

Just as in the rest of the Middle East, Egyptian desserts tend to be either syrup-soaked pastries or milk-based puddings. Examples of the former include *basboosa*, semolina cake soaked in syrup; *ka'ab al-ghazaal* (literally 'gazelle horns'), horn-shaped pastries filled with almonds and soaked in orange water; *luqmat al-gaadee*, fried dough balls in syrup; and *qataayaf*, similar to baklava. Examples of the latter include the ubiquitous *mahlabeeya*, a kind of rice pudding, and the celebrated *umm ali* (literally, 'Ali's Mum'), a very rich type of bread-and-butter pudding made with nuts, raisins and spices.

WHERE AND WHEN TO EAT

Egyptian eateries range from the type of top-end (in price and quality) international restaurants that are usually found in five-star hotels, to Middle Eastern-style restaurants targeting tourists, and local fast-food joints (such as the ubiquitous but wildly popular chain, *Gad*) and simple street stalls. Don't dismiss these last, however: they are often open 24 hours a day in the towns and offer felafel sandwiches, *shwarmas* (doner kebabs) or *fiteers* (a kind of local pizza) that can't be beaten after a long journey, a night out or if you're too late to get food at a restaurant. Made to order from fresh ingredients, they're often a safer bet than hotel buffet food.

Egyptians usually eat late, well into the afternoon at lunchtime, and from 9pm, 10pm or later for dinner; at weekends, meals may often be even later.

DRINKS

Hot Drinks

Cafés commonly serve *shay* (tea) drunk with milk and lots of sugar, or *bilnaana* (with mint), as well as *'ahwa* (Egyptian coffee, which is similar to Turkish coffee). Order it *sukkar wasat* or *mazboot* (sweetened), *sukkar ziyaada* (extra sweet) or *saada* (without sugar). Western-style coffee is referred to as *'ahwa amreekiyya* (American coffee).

Worth tasting also are herbal infusions such as *helba* (fenugreek), *yansoon* (anis) or *irfa* (cinnamon), and in winter, *sahlab* (a hot milky mixture of arrowroot or semolina, nuts and cinnamon and sometimes raisins).

In Upper Egypt you will often find *karkadeh*, a refreshing hot (or cold) infusion of hibiscus flowers that is supposed to help raise (if served hot) or lower (when cold) your blood pressure. This is often served by Egyptian hotels for breakfast or for refreshment.

Cold Drinks

Bottled water is widely available in Egypt and is cheap, as are soft drinks such as Coca-Cola. A surprisingly refreshing local drink popular in summer is *zabaady*, a yogurt-based drink diluted with water and salt.

Egyptians adore fresh juices *(asir)*, and many juice bars line the towns' streets; they're easily spotted by the pyramids of seasonal fruit piled up in front.

Orange *(burtuaan)*, mango *(manga)*, banana *(muz)*, lemon *(limoon)*, apple *(tufaah)*, sugar cane *(asab)* and sometimes tamarind *(tamr hindee)* are commonly found.

Alcoholic Drinks

Most Egyptians are Muslims and, strictly speaking, forbidden from drinking alcohol by the Qur'an, but alcohol is still widely available in Cairo and other tourist centres.

There are several varieties of decent-quality locally brewed beer, including *Stella* and the newer *Sakkara*, as well as more expensive imported brands.

Several companies produce wine in Egypt. including red, white and rosé *Gianaclis*, made from grapes grown near Alexandria, and red, white and rosé *Obélisque* produced on the Red Sea Coast from concentrated grape juice imported from Europe. *Grand de Marquise* is probably the best of the bunch, which produces a reasonably drinkable red and white. Imported wines are not easily available (except in upper-range hotels), and are very expensive.

Above from far left: selling vegetables in one of Cairo's souqs; taking a tea break.

Eating Etiquette

If you are invited to an Egyptian home, it's considered polite to bring a gift such as pastries, sweets or flowers. When entering an Egyptian house, remember to remove your shoes, as this is standard etiquette. Wash your hands when your host offers, and, if you are not shown to your seat, sit down next to someone of the same sex. When eating, try to use only your right hand to eat (the left is reserved for ablutions), and try to avoid showing the soles of your feet to your host. Greed (such as overly reaching for food, particularly for dishes that aren't placed in front of you) and guzzling are considered bad manners, but so is refusing at least some second helpings (which will be forced repeatedly upon you). Once you are genuinely full, place your right hand over your stomach or heart to demonstrate repletion and thanks. During Ramadan, avoiding eating, drinking or smoking in public shows sensitivity, consideration and respect.

SHOPPING

There's no shortage of retail opportunities in Egypt. Though most shops and stalls in towns along the Nile sell souvenirs including some fabulous 'pharaonic kitsch', better-quality, more original artefacts are not too hard to find. A foray into the towns' souqs, where the locals shop, is well worthwhile.

Many towns along the Nile, including Luxor, Aswan and Abu Simbel, owe their continued existence and livelihood to tourism. The rows of shops and stalls, as well as the waves of itinerant vendors and touts – usually very dogged – form both the best and worst memories of visitors' trips.

If you're not interested in buying, a firm '*La, shukran*' ('No thank you' in Arabic) and the avoidance of eye contact with either the vendor or the object for sale usually does the trick.

If you are interested in buying, the secret is to take your time and enjoy it *(see margin, p.21, and feature, p.21).*

SOUQS

One experience that is worthwhile but which is sometimes overlooked by visitors is a foray into the town souqs. One of the oldest and greatest social, cultural and economic traditions of the Middle East, souqs are where the Egyptians do their shopping, and where also you'll get a real glimpse of Egyptian daily life. If you're feeling nervous of heading out alone, ask your hotel to send someone to accompany you (in return for a small tip).

Selling everything from pungent spices to exotic vegetables and fruits,

Right: interior of a fez shop.

plus camels, *gallabiyyas* (traditional Egyptian floor-length 'shirts') and reams of cloth, the souqs are a great place to browse, particularly in the cool of the evening when people from all walks of life appear to be out exchanging news and gossip, running errands, transacting business and shopping for dinner.

Souqs tend to be divided by the products on sale, so you'll find the spice stalls all in one area, fabrics in another, etc – all the easier for browsing and comparing prices.

WHAT TO BUY AND WHERE

Quality can be hard to come by, so allow plenty of time for shopping. Cairo is the best place for making purchases in terms of both quality and price, though original, decent-quality and reasonably priced goods can be found elsewhere. Aswan is a good place in particular for genuine Nubian arts and crafts.

Antiques and Antiquities

You need a licence from the Department of Antiquities to export genuine pharaonic, Islamic and Coptic antiques; this should be obtained by the dealer. Be aware, though, that most antiquities on offer are fake. The best place to hunt for antiques is Cairo, especially the Khan Al Khalili Bazaar *(see p.40)*.

Handicrafts

The best place to buy arts and crafts at good prices, of good quality and from a wide selection is also the Khan Al Khalili in Cairo, as well the souqs of Luxor and Aswan. Products include copper and brassware, *sheesha* pipes and traditional musical instruments.

Good buys in Cairo include hand-painted papyrus, as well as carved wooden objects with intricate mother-of-pearl inlay work (such as backgammon and chess sets), and hand-blown recycled *muski* glass.

For the former, try Dr Ragab's Papyrus Institute (near the Cairo Sheraton, Corniche An Nil, Giza), where demonstrations of traditional papyrus-making can be seen, and high-quality products (albeit not the cheapest) are sold. Elsewhere, beware the banana-leaf imitations, which are ubiquitous but also difficult for the untrained eye to detect.

Luxor boasts several good alabaster workshops on the West Bank, where you can see the stone being worked and polished. Products range from the kitsch statuettes and sphinxes that are finished with a light sheen, to the polished and unpolished alabaster vases or bowls, not unlike the ones on show in the Egyptian Museum in Cairo.

In Luxor, two shops worth singling out are: the Fair Trade Centre Luxor Outlet (Shari' Al Karnak), which sells handicrafts issuing from NGO projects based in the Luxor region,

Above from far left: textiles at market in Cairo; jewellery in the ancient style.

Credit Cards and Cash
In tourist areas and large hotels, most shops accept major credit cards and travellers' cheques for larger purchases, but smaller shops often accept only cash (though they sometimes take dollars, euros or pounds sterling).

Below: Cairo souq.

as well as good aromatic oils, and the Australian-run Habiba (Sharia Sidi Mahmoud, off Sharia As Souq), which sells a selection of decent-quality Egyptian handicrafts, including small embroidered evening bags, Siwan scarves and Egyptian cotton towels.

In Aswan, a good shop for Nubian jewellery and objects is Hanafi Bazaar, located in a mock pharaonic temple on the Corniche An Nil.

Egyptian Cotton and Other Fabrics

Egyptian cotton is world famous, but it can be hard to find decent-quality products in Egypt itself because much of it is exported. Inexpensive, locally made cotton fabrics and garments are abundant, however, so many visitors take advantage to stock up on T-shirts, thin cotton trousers and other casual wear, which are good in the heat.

Traditional Egyptian clothes including *gallabiyyas,* which some visitors like to buy as light dressing gowns or to put over swimwear, are found in Cairo's Khan Al Khalili Bazaar or in the souqs of Luxor and Aswan.

Other traditional items range from cushion covers or wall hangings made with appliqué work to attractive pottery, and even belly-dancer outfits.

Jewellery

Many Egyptian women still consider the ownership of gold jewellery as a safer form of saving than owning a bank account. Every souq has a good jewellery section, and gifts of jewellery form an important part of many social rituals, including courtship and marriage. Most gold jewellery is made from 18-carat gold, but Bedouin women, and ladies from the countryside, prefer the brighter but softer 21-carat gold.

Gold and silver are sold by the gram; the daily rates are printed in the *Egyptian Gazette,* among other papers in Egypt. An additional fee for the workmanship is added to the price, but as labour is cheap in Egypt,

jewellery is usually much better value here in Europe or the US. One popular purchase easily found in Cairo are gold or silver cartouches engraved with the visitor's name in hieroglyphics.

Three recommended jewellery shops in Cairo are: Nomad Gallery (14 Saraya Al Gezira, 1st floor, Zamalik, or the smaller shop at the Cairo Marriott), which sells well-made copies of Bedouin jewellery; the Al Ain Gallery (73 Shari' Al Hussain, Doqqi) or the First Mall in Giza (tel: 02-2573 7687) which belong to Egyptian designer Azza Fahmy and sell beautiful jewellery inspired by traditional designs; and the Sheba Gallery (6 Shari' Sri Lanka in Zamalik; www.shebagallery. com), which sells highly original and creative designs in silver and gold.

Perfumes

Egypt produces several pure essences for the Western perfume market. Sold by the ounce, they are then diluted with alcohol to make perfume. Be aware that although some shopkeepers offer the real thing, many add vegetable oil to the essence instead, and often overcharge also.

Some perfumeries can custom-make an essence for you, or can try to copy your favourite perfume.

Spices

Inexpensive, often good-quality and lightweight, spices make great sou-

venirs or gifts to take home. Choose a seller that's popular with locals and opt for spices produced locally (ideally in the area you are in), such as cumin, coriander, black pepper and red chilli. Saffron or green pepper, which are usually imported, can lack both flavour and colour (and are expensive).

Aswan is famous for peanuts and *karkadeh* (dried hibiscus flowers), which the locals use to make a refreshing drink *(see p.17)*.

OPENING TIMES

Shops and souqs generally open from Saturday to Thursday from 9am to 1pm and 5pm to 10pm in summer and 10am to 6pm in winter.

Retail Rituals

Shopping in Egypt is a slower and more elaborate process than in the West. The age-old and intricate rituals include the exchanging of greetings and enquiring after respective families, the sipping of copious cups of tea, the fingering and discussing of products at length, and, last but not least, negotiating and agreeing on a price *(see box, below)*.

The Art of Haggling

Bar in tourist shops and hotels, few prices are ever fixed. Though Western visitors may be unused to haggling and uncomfortable with it, the secret is to get stuck in and enjoy it! In fact, it's a more equitable system that it may seem, since every purchaser/vendor ends up buying/selling at the price he/she can afford. Here are a few tips: if you see something you like, check it out in a few shops until you have an idea of its worth. Never open the negotiations; wait for the vendor to offer first. When he/she does, offer around a third of the asking price then be prepared to settle for slightly over half. If the trader refuses to bargain, make to walk away. If your offer was good, he/she will follow you dropping the price as you walk further away. Never enter into bargaining if you don't intend to buy, and always pay the final agreed price.

ENTERTAINMENT

Few travellers visit Egypt for its entertainment scene, but the latter has a prestigious heritage, with belly dancers, performance artists and musicians all having diverted the pharaohs. Within the Arab world, too, Egypt is well known for its vast and prolific film and music industries.

Mention Egypt and entertainment, and most people will think of belly dancing. There's much more here for the culturally curious, however.

FILM

Spectacular Vision
Egypt's famous Sound and Light Shows are staged at some of the Nile's most famous monuments: Cairo's pyramids of Giza; Luxor's Karnak Temple; Philae's temple near Aswan, and Abu Simbel's temple. They usually last 60–90 minutes and cost around LE100. Some are sounding a little dated; all of them are kitsch; for some they bring the pharaohs back to life, and also offer a unique chance to wander the monuments at night. The illuminated pyramids in particular make a spectacular sight.

Three-quarters of all films made in the Arab world come from Egypt. Like the music industry, Egypt's film industry had its heyday in the 1940s and '50s, when up to 100 films were produced annually. The industry was nationalised in the 1950s, and a combination of heavy censorship and taxation, plus a general drop in standards of production, have seen both output and quality drop dramatically. Recently, signs of a revival have started to show.

An Egyptian film-maker much honoured in international film festivals, and known as 'the Fellini of Egypt', is the Alexandrine Youssef Chahine (1926–2008). Other prolific directors include Youssef Wahbi (1898–1982) and Yousry Nasrallah (b.1952).

Among the best-known features shot on the Nile include Agatha Christie's *Death on the Nile* (1978), set on a cruise steamship, as well as the *Spy Who Loved Me* (1977), which was shot around the pyramids, medieval Cairo and Luxor. *Gallipoli* (1981) was partly set in Cairo, as was *Sphinx* (1980), based on the best-selling novel by Peter Cook.

FESTIVALS

Dates of the Nile's major festivals vary (check with the Tourist Office *(see p.107)* for full details) but include:

January
Cairo International Book Fair (Cairo Exhibition Grounds; tel: 02-2575 4069). One of the world's largest fairs.

February
Ascension of Rameses II, Abu Simbel: 22 February *(see p.91).*
Luxor Marathon (www.egyptian marathon.net).
Al Nitaq (Downtown Cairo). Vibrant, multi-venue arts festival.

June
International Festival of Oriental Dance (Cairo; www.nilegroup.net). Performances and instruction in the art of belly dancing.

September

International Festival for Experimental Theatre, Cairo.

Alexandria International Film Festival (tel: 03-576 8727; www.alexandriafilmfestival.com).

October

Pharaohs' Rally (Siag Travel: 02-2385 2626). An 11-day, motorbike and four-wheel-drive desert race, beginning and ending at the pyramids.

Birth of Rameses II, Abu Simbel: 22 October *(see p.91)*.

November

Arab Music Festival (Cairo Opera House). A 10-day festival of classical and traditional Arabic music.

December

Cairo International Film Festival (tel: 02-2392 3962; www.cairofilmfestival.com).

MUSIC

The 1940s and '50s were considered Egypt's golden age of music. Epitomising the era above all was the 'Star of the East' and national icon, Umm Kolthum (1904–75), considered to be the greatest Arab singer of the 20th century. A museum (Umm Kolthum Museum in Cairo) and a suite at the Mena Palace Hotel (Cairo), where she used to stay following her legendary concerts, are dedicated to her. You can buy her recordings in Cairo (as well as download them from iTunes).

Popular Egyptian music icons include Ahmed Adawiyya, active in the 1970s, who is also credited with spawning two peculiarly Egyptian pop styles since, *Al Jeel* ('The Generation') and *Shaabi* ('Popular').

Amr Diab, known as the 'Arab Ricky Martin', is a contemporary star, popular for his Western-style pop; his album *Nour El Ain* is the biggest-grossing album of the Arab world.

Egypt has the best production facilities (for both music and film) in the Arab World, as well as one of its liveliest cultural scenes. A number of institutions and cultural centres also benefit from state and international funding.

THEATRE AND BALLET

The main venue is the Cairo Opera House (Gezira Exhibition Grounds; tel: 02-2739 8444), which also hosts Egyptian and international orchestral recitals, modern dance performances and musicals. For performances in the main hall, jacket and tie are required. Egyptian theatre is mostly in Arabic and concentrated in Cairo.

TRADITIONAL DANCE

Belly dancing is thought to have originated in Egypt *(see margin, right)* and Cairo is considered the best place in the world to see it.

Above from far left: whirling dervish; traditional musicians at Kom Umbu Temple; belly dancer in full swing.

Belly Dancers
The source of erotic titillation for some, a toe-curling hazard for others are Egypt's belly dancers. Though they appear to cater only to tourists and to feed orientalist fantasies, the art of belly dancing (as it is indeed considered by its practitioners) is an ancient one, dating back to pharaonic times and flourishing throughout the medieval period in the form of the *ghawazee* (similar to European troubadours). Today's performers attract Egyptians as well as tourists; the best can be found in the top hotels and on the upmarket cruise ships.

EGYPT'S KEY PHARAOHS

Thanks to the pyramids, tombs and other major monuments left behind by the pharaohs, Ancient Egypt has become almost synonymous with them. This chronology includes some of the principal players.

Meaning 'great abode', the term pharaoh derives from the palaces the kings inhabited. All-powerful, the pharaohs controlled political, military, religious and social life, and later came to be worshipped as gods incarnate by their people. Usually, the title of pharaoh passed from father to eldest son via the Chief Consort, creating Ancient Egypt's many different dynasties. The following list includes some of the key characters. Brackets following names give alternative names, very approximate reigns, dynasties and capital cities.

OLD KINGDOM (DYNASTIES III–VI) 2663–2195 BC

Djoser *(Zoser; c.2654–c.2635 BC; 3rd Dynasty; Memphis)*
Making Memphis his capital, Djoser probably extended Egypt's southern and eastern borders. Following a seven-year famine, Djoser dedicated a temple to Khnum *(see p.27)* on Elephantine Island, Aswan, and most famously, erected the Step Pyramid at Saqarah, near Memphis, Egypt's first (and the world's earliest) wholly stone-made, monumental building.

Khufu *(Cheops; c.2547–c.2524 BC; 4th Dynasty; Memphis)*
Though the Greek historian Herodotus records that Khufu and his son, Khafra, were despotic and cruel, Khufu is credited with military expeditions to Nubia, Libya and Sinai, the centralisation of the state, the curbing of the powers of the priests and, most famously, the erection of the Great Pyramid at Giza.

Khafra *(Khafre, Chephren, Khephren; c.2516–c.2493 BC; 4th Dynasty; Memphis)*
Khafra is most famous as the builder of some of Egypt's most impressive monuments. These include his pyramid at Giza and the Sphinx, whose face was reputedly modelled on Khafra's.

NEW KINGDOM (DYNASTIES XVIII–XX), 1550–1064 BC

Thutmose III *(Thutmoses, Thutmosis; c.1479–c.1425 BC; 18th Dynasty; Memphis)*
Reclaiming the throne after the death of his much-resented stepmother, Hatshepsut (whose memory he tried to erase by defacing her monuments), Thutmose is also known as 'Egypt's

Napoleon' for his military brilliance and his great conquests in the south and east, including against the Nubians, Assyrians and Canaanites.

Hatshepsut *(c.1472–c.1457 BC; 18th Dynasty; Thebes)*

On the death of her husband, Thutmose II, Hatshepsut ruled as regent but later had herself crowned pharaoh, even donning the traditional false beard and kilt and sidelining her stepson, Thutmose III. She achieved military conquests in Libya, the Levant and Nubia, re-established important trading routes and undertook a bountiful expedition to the Land of Punt (recorded on her famous mortuary temple at Dair Al Bahari, *see p.73*).

Akhenaten *(c.1360–c.1343 BC; 18th Dynasty; Akhetaten, modern-day Al Amarnah)*

Dubbed the 'heretical pharaoh', Akhenaten changed his name from Amenhotep IV, abandoned Thebes and created a new capital at Al Amarnah, and introduced the new cult of the sun-god Aten, replacing the god Amun and the old order. Successive pharaohs restored the old state religion and tried to erase his name from history. Nefertiti was his wife.

Tutankhamun *(c.1343–c.1333 BC; 18th Dynasty; Thebes)*

World-famous for the treasures of his tomb, Tutankhamun's reign was neither long nor particularly distinguished. He did reintroduce the old cult of Amun, restore the privileges of the priests and re-establish the old capital of Thebes after Akhenaten's controversial reign. He died at the age of 19, weakened – according to the very latest recent theories – by the combination of a fall and malaria.

Sety I *(Seti, Sethos; c.1296–c.1279 BC; 19th Dynasty; Memphis)*

Considered to be one of Egypt's great warrior-pharaohs, Sety I boasted military victories against the Hittites and Canaanites among others, and erected a number of monumental buildings, including Karnak's hypostyle hall (which was completed by his son, Rameses II) and temples at Abydos and Thebes.

Rameses II *(c.1279–c.1212 BC; 19th Dynasty; Pi-Ramesse, near modern-day Al Khatana)*

Rameses II is also known as Rameses the Great after his numerous military expeditions in Nubia, Libya and Syria, including the Battle of Kadesh in 1274 BC, following which he signed the world's first peace treaty with the Hittites. He is also famous as the great builder of many of Egypt's most impressive monuments including the temples at Abu Simbel, the Ramesseum and the Colossus at Memphis. He reputedly fathered over 200 children and died in his 90s.

Above from far left:
Djoser; the Sphinx and pyramids at Giza; Akhenaten.

Other Dynasties
- Early Dynastic period (1st and 2nd dynasties), 3050–2663 BC
- First Intermediate period (7th–10th dynasties), 2195–2160 BC
- Middle Kingdom (11th and 12th dynasties), 2160–1650 BC
- Second Intermediate period (13th–17th dynasties), 1650–1550 BC
- Third Intermediate period (21st–25th dynasties), 1064–656 BC
- Saite period (26th Dynasty), 664–525 BC
- Persian and Macedonian rule (27th–31st dynasties) 525–332 BC
- Invasion of Alexander the Great (Dynasty of Macedonia), 332 BC
- Ptolemaic period (Dynasty of the Ptolemies) 310–30 BC
- Cleopatra VII (51–30 BC; Dynasty of Ptolemy; Alexandria; *see p.63*)
- Roman period 30 BC–395 AD

ANCIENT EGYPT'S GODS

The Ancient Egyptians worshipped over 2,000 gods. Each had their own role and domain of responsibility, as well their own personality, cult and mythology. Walking around Egypt's ancient monuments, however, you'll come across the same major deities again and again. Here's a quick guide.

ANUBIS

Serving as the conveyor of souls of the dead, Anubis was also connected with the rituals of mummification, the weighing of hearts and protection of the mummies. He is usually depicted (often on one of the four canopic jars) as a man with a jackal's head, or as a recumbent jackal, fox or dog.

BASTET (BAST)

Daughter of Ra *(see opposite)*, Bastet was associated with the ripening of crops and was also the goddess of cats (sacred to the Ancient Egyptians), the household, merriment and music. She is depicted as half woman with the head of a cat and holding a *sistrum* (rattle-like musical instrument).

HATHOR

Goddess of joy, pleasure, festivities, dancing, love and women, Hathor was shown as a woman with cow ears; sometimes horns, with a sun disc between; or a cow's head. She was considered the quintessence of beauty. Dandarah was an important centre of her cult.

HORUS

Son of Osiris and Isis *(see opposite and below)*, Horus was one of Ancient Egypt's key gods. After his uncle, Seth *(see opposite)*, slayed his father, Horus defeated Seth and reclaimed the throne of Egypt. Prince of gods and god of the skies, he is usually depicted as a falcon wearing the double crown of Egypt or as half human with a falcon head. Horus was the patron of the pharaoh and was also invoked to protect people from dangerous daily hazards such as scorpions, cobras and crocodiles.

ISIS

Wife and sister of Osiris and mother of Horus, Isis was worshipped principally as a mother-goddess, but also as the great protector. Symbolising the ideal mother and wife, she became one of the most popular goddesses in Egypt and elsewhere. Isis is portrayed as a woman with large, outstretched wings (protecting the dead from evil); standing holding a sceptre, with a sun between two horns; sitting suckling her son Horus, or kneeling beside the sarcophagus of her dead husband,

Divine Images
Once inhabiting the inner sanctum of the temples were magnificent solid gold or silver images of the gods. Washed and anointed before festivals, they were brought out to dazzle and overawe the populace. Sadly, over the successive centuries they have been plundered and melted down, and very few remain.

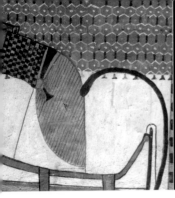

Osiris. Temples at Philae and Dandarah are dedicated to her.

KHNUM

Associated with the annual flooding of the Nile, Khnum was the god of fertility. He is represented as half man with a ram's head with long, flat horns, and was venerated at Esna.

OSIRIS

One of the principal gods of Ancient Egypt, Osiris was god of the dead and the underworld. Son of Geb (the earth-god) and Nut (the sky-goddess), Osiris was murdered by his evil and jealous brother, Seth, but was later brought back to life by Isis, his wife and sister. He symbolised life after death as well as regeneration after the annual flooding of the Nile. Osiris is usually portrayed wearing a crown of two ostrich feathers between a bundle of reeds, with a small plaited beard, and clutching a ceremonial flail and crook, symbols of kingship. At Edfu, a temple is dedicated to him.

RA (RE)

King of the gods, lord of all creation and supreme judge was the sun-god, Ra. From the 5th Dynasty, every pharaoh claimed to be Ra's son and his living incarnation on earth. Every day, Ra would journey across the sky in his solar boat, be consumed at dusk by the sky-goddess Nut, travel through the underworld, and later resurrect himself (and life) the next morning.

Ra oversaw the fertility of the soil and escorted deceased pharaohs in their barges to the underworld. Ra was later amalgamated with other gods such as Amun-Ra, Ra-Horakhty and Min-Ra.

He is commonly depicted as a human with a falcon or ram's head bearing a sun disc.

SETH

Usurping the throne of Egypt from his brother, Osiris, before defeat at the hands of Horus, Seth represented evil, disorder and chaos. He is usually depicted as half human with an aardvark-like head, or sometimes as a hippopotamus, snake-like dragon, crocodile, dog or pig. Christian Egypt portrayed him as the devil, complete with forked tail. He is often depicted near the sun-god's boat, as it journeys through the underworld.

THOTH

Credited with the invention of hieroglyphics and language, medicine and mathematics, Thoth was god of healing and wisdom, as well as god of the moon. He was depicted as a man with the head of an ibis or as a baboon.

Above from far left: image of Hathor at the Temple of Hatshepsut, Dair Al Bahari; Anubis, shown here (as usual), as a man with a jackal's head; statues of Rameses II as Osiris in Karnak Temple, Luxor.

Pharaonic Influence Christian symbols such as the cross very probably developed from the sacred symbol of the *ankh*; the cult of the Virgin from the wildly popular cult of Isis, still worshipped in Egypt for 200 years after the advent of Christianity.

ARCHITECTURE OF THE PHARAOHS

The gods and goddesses played a vital part in the daily lives of the Ancient Egyptians. To curry divine favour for their people on earth as well as themselves in the afterlife, the pharaohs constructed temples in honour of the gods, as well as tombs and pyramids for their own eternal divinity.

Herodotus, the Greek historian who visited Egypt in 450 BC, wrote that the Egyptians were 'religious to excess, beyond any other nation in the world'. Since his time, visitors have been struck dumb by the remains of these monumental religious constructions. However, many of these buildings in fact share many features and follow a common design.

TEMPLES

Ancient Egyptian temples physically and symbolically represented the house of the god that was venerated. They are of two main styles: the open-air, solar temples of the Old Kingdom (which dates from *c.*2663 BC), few traces of which remain, and the enclosed, 'classic' temples, found from the New Kingdom onwards (dating from *c.*1550 BC).

Some of the most famous examples of the latter can be found along the Nile at the temples of Karnak, Luxor, Abydos, Dandarah, Edfu and Abu Simbel.

Design and Decoration

At the entrance of most classic temples stood a monumental entrance gateway known as a pylon, which symbolised the horizon. Behind the pylon lay an open-air courtyard, followed usually by one or more further pylons, slightly smaller each time than the first, sometimes along with further courtyards.

Beyond the pylons and courtyards lay the hypostyle, a hall filled with columns that supported a decorated ceiling under a flat roof.

After the hypostyle, one or more small offering halls would lead to the inner sanctum, also known as the Holy of Holies. It was here that the sacred image of the god to whom the temple was dedicated was kept (see p.26).

The entire temple was decorated with statues of gods (regrettably very few are found in situ today), as well as brightly painted plaster reliefs (see p.31).

Purpose

Over time, the temples developed into whole complexes with offices, food stores, shops, schools, libraries

Quarrying and Transportation

How Ancient Egypt quarried, carved and transported stone for its great monuments has long mystified visitors. In a nutshell, quarriers would demarcate the size and shape of the block by chiselling an outline. Wooded wedges were then inserted along the outline and doused with water until they expanded, shattering and separating the stone from the rock face. Using the annual Nile floods, the blocks were then transported from the quarries to the monument site submerged between two boats, reducing their weight by a third.

Above from far left: the Temple of Horus at Edfu from afar and close up.

and quarters of the priesthood all surrounding the building, serving not just the spiritual but also the political and economic needs of the area.

For the New Kingdom pharaohs, the temples came to serve three principal purposes: as places for the worship (and placation) of the gods, centres to raise and collect tax (the people would come here to pay their annual dues according to measurements of the Nilometers *(see margin, p.80)*, and as political propaganda.

For the latter purpose, many of the carvings attempt to legitimise the pharaoh's power by showing him consorting with and receiving blessings from the gods, as well as portraying his great victories over his enemies or those foolish enough to rebel against him.

TOMBS

Land of the Dead

Flowing south to north, the Nile divides Egypt into east and west. As the Ancient Egyptians saw it, the sun rose each day on the east bank and died every night on the west. Accordingly, they largely inhabited the east, the land of the living, and buried the deceased on the west bank in the land of the dead. The crossing of the Nile symbolised the journey to meet the sun-god.

Tomb Types

Early Egyptians interred their dead in simple burial pits in the desert outside the perimeters of their settlements. Later, high-ranking families were buried in shallow graves lined with mud bricks or stones, which were known as mastabas.

Later still, during the 3rd Dynasty (*c.*2700–2600 BC) and for around 500 years, pharaohs and other high-ranking officials had huge stone pyramids built, including those found today at Giza and Memphis. Nearby, mastabas housed the pharaoh's servants, families and friends (these can also be seen at Giza).

From around 2150 BC, and for approximately another 500 years, Egypt's rulers chose to be buried in underground chambers in the Valley of the Kings and Valley of the Queens on the West Bank of modern-day Luxor, the site of Ancient Thebes, and the then capital of Egypt.

Royal Regalia

Pharaohs of Lower Egypt (today's northern Egypt) wore a red, bucket-like crown, while the kings of Upper Egypt (the south) wore a white, bottle-like crown. When the two regions were united *(see p.32)*, the two crowns were amalgamated by artists to look like 'a bottle of champagne in an ice bucket', as Egypt's guides like to put it. Other royal garb included a crook and flail (to identify with Osiris, king of the gods and father of pharaohs), a false beard (since the gods were thought to be bearded), a medallion-like decoration on the crown representing either a cobra (the goddess of Lower Egypt) or vulture (goddess of Upper Egypt) and a *nemes* (striped headdress).

PYRAMIDS

The remains of over 123 pyramids have so far been found in Egypt. Acting like giant billboards, they advertised to the world the might of the pharaohs. However, as the power of the kings declined, so also did the pyramid-building, with fewer and less well-constructed pyramids occurring after the end of the third millennium BC.

Exterior Design

The first, Djoser's Step Pyramid, was built in the 27th century BC. Its six steps culminating in a flat top were thought to have acted symbolically as a staircase to heaven for the king's spirit. Subsequent pyramids were smooth-sided.

The immense size of the pyramids combined with the blinding-white limestone that once covered them, would have astonished onlookers. Very little of the limestone facing remains; it was removed in the Roman period and ground into powder for mortar, and later during medieval times for the construction of mosques.

Interior Design

Inside the sand-, stone- and rubble-filled pyramids, reinforced passageways led to one or several burial chambers where the pharaoh and perhaps also members of his family were buried.

False passages and chambers were sometimes constructed to mislead tomb robbers, who posed a problem even in the pharaohs' day. The last workers left via an escape passage and both entrances were then carefully concealed.

Decoration

Inside the tombs, decoration could be sophisticated or crude, elaborate or

Below: interior of the Temple of Dandarah.

even unfinished (if, for example, the pharaoh died prematurely), depending upon the power and prestige of the pharaoh and his kingdom.

Tomb paintings tell us a great deal about Ancient Egypt, its religion and rituals, culture and society, as well as the life of the pharaohs, the priests and the ordinary people.

Tomb Treasures

Tombs were filled not just with precious treasures such as jewellery and gold funerary ornaments, but also with everyday objects that were thought to be useful to the pharaoh in the afterlife, including food, cosmetics, beds, incense, clothing, chariots and weapons. Tutankhamun's tomb included his favourite toys and even underpants.

Models of servants (called *shabtis*) were also included in the tomb, sometimes several hundred at a time, that would come to life to perform all the menial tasks for the pharaoh in the afterlife. Finally, the four canopic jars were placed in the burial chamber.

Building Tools and Techniques

In the absence of advanced tools and technology (the wheel, along with iron, was not introduced into Egypt until much later, and softer copper tools were used instead) the Ancient Egyptians relied on two things they did have: manpower and good organisational skills.

The vast blocks of stone *(see margin, p.28)* were transported over land using sledges or wooden rollers pulled by teams of men, and sometimes animals too.

Water channels were used to check the land was level, ramps of sand were constructed to increase the height of the pyramid, and simple systems of levers were used to raise the blocks into place.

Interior Decor
After the temple was built, wall surfaces were smoothed down, plaster applied and left to dry. Artists would then mark out in black ink designs copied from papyrus blueprints. After inspection by a master draughtsman who would mark corrections with a red pen, carvers would set to work. On exterior walls, drawings were chiselled in sunken or bas-relief to survive the weather better; on interior walls they were carved in raised relief. After painting, they were glazed with egg white or honey-based mixtures.

Building Ancient Egypt

Egypt's earliest abodes were made of sticks, wattle and daub. Mud brick began to appear as early as 4000 BC in the construction of important buildings. Nobles and kings were buried in brick and wood-lined, shallow graves. Around 3000 BC, the pharaohs began to choose stone over brick, as they sought to create 'eternal palaces', which led to the building of the world's first pyramid, Djoser's stepped pyramid at Saqarah dating to around 2700 BC. Thereafter, right up until Roman times, stone (mainly sandstone, but also limestone and granite) was used for all pharaonic funerary architecture, while brick was employed for domestic architecture and the construction of the towns.

HISTORY: KEY DATES

Few countries boast a richer and more colourful history than Egypt. Mesopotamians, Greeks, Romans, Arabs, Ottomans and Europeans have all passed through its portals and left their mark upon the country.

FIRST SETTLERS AND PREHISTORIC AND DYNASTIC PERIODS

Ancient Geography
In Ancient Egypt, the country was divided into two geopolitical regions: 'Lower Egypt' denoted the north of Egypt, stretching from beyond the Nile Delta to south of modern-day Cairo; 'Upper Egypt' referred to the area lying south of Cairo all the way to the First Cataract in Aswan.

250,000 BC	Earliest traces of human habitation in Egypt. Desertification forces hunter-gathers to settle the Nile.
3100 BC	Unification of Upper and Lower Egypt *(see margin, left)* by King Menes (Narmer) marks the beginning of the Dynastic period.
2663–2195 BC	The Old Kingdom sees the country's wealth and power expand. Art, science and architecture reach new heights. Construction of the Step Pyramid in Saqarah and Giza's Great Pyramid.
1550–1064 BC	After 600 years of decline, New Kingdom pharaohs re-establish Egypt's power in the region, assuring wealth and stability again.
1360–1343 BC	Amenhotep IV and his wife Nefertiti found a new capital at Al Amarnah and introduce the worship of the god Aten.
1343 BC	The boy king Tutankhaten restores order and changes his name to Tutankhamun.
1296–1279 BC	Sety I leads an Egyptian Renaissance. Despite the military successes of his son, Rameses II, the empire is in terminal decline.

GREEK AND ROMAN RULE

331 BC	Macedonian general Alexander the Great founds a new capital at Alexandria, opening Egypt up to the Mediterranean world.
31 BC	Cleopatra VII commits suicide after her and Mark Antony's defeat by Octavian (later the Emperor Augustus) at the Battle of Actium. Egypt becomes a Roman province.
AD 45	St Mark brings Christianity to Egypt.

ARAB, EUROPEAN AND OTTOMAN RULE

641	The arab Amr Ibn Al As conquers Egypt and introduces Islam.
969	The Fatimids found the city of Al Qahirah (Cairo).

1171–93	Salah Addin (Saladin) rules Egypt and regains both Syria and Jerusalem from the Crusaders.
1517	As an Ottoman province Egypt begins a long economic decline.
1798	Recognising Egypt's strategic importance positioned between Europe and the East, Napoleon Bonaparte invades Egypt and declares it a French protectorate until defeat by the British.
1805	The reformist Albanian Muhammad Ali, considered the founder of modern Egypt, takes over.

MODERN EGYPT

1869	Khedive Ismail opens the Suez Canal, creating a passage between the Mediterranean and the Red Sea.
1883–1922	Egypt is Britain's 'Veiled Protectorate', under British control.
1952	King Farouk is overthrown by the army in a bloodless coup.
1953	On 26 July, Egypt is declared a republic, and Gamal Abd An Nasser *(see margin, right)* becomes president.
1956	Nasser's nationalisation of the Suez Canal sparks an invasion of British, French and Israeli forces.
1978	President Anwar As Sadat recognises Israel's right to exist in the Camp David Peace Accord.
1981	President As Sadat is assassinated: Hosni Mubarak takes over as president and attempts to stem the growing influence of Muslim fundamentalists.
1990s	Egypt is hit by terrorist activities of Muslim extremists, who target foreign tourists, culminating in the Dair Al Bahari (Luxor) attack in 1997, when 58 tourists are killed.
2005	After yielding to US pressure to permit other election candidates, President Mubarak wins a convincing victory, which sees his fifth term and 25th year extended to 2011.
2009	Mubarak forges peace talks between Israel and the Palestinians over Gaza. US President Obama delivers an historic speech in Cairo addressed to the Muslim world; Egypt's key role as regional mediator is confirmed.
2010	Egypt becomes the first nation to win the Africa of Nations Cup three times in a row. In June, a new East African-proposed water-sharing treaty is vetoed by Sudan and Egypt, reigniting an old, ever-more dangerous dispute among the Nile Basin countries.

Above from far left: invasion of Egypt by the British in 1882 resulted in British control from 1883 to 1922; the Suez Canal *c*.1856–60, prior to its opening to shipping in 1869.

Gamal Abd An Nasser
Leader of the Free Officers that toppled the British-backed King Farouk, Gamal Abd An Nasser (1918–70) set about introducing a major modernisation and social reform programme. When denied US funding for the building of the Aswan High Dam, he nationalised the Suez Canal then faced down the combined forces of Britain, France and Israel. Hailed as Egypt's greatest statesman, he's also the father of pan-Arab nationalism and one of the key figures in modern political history.

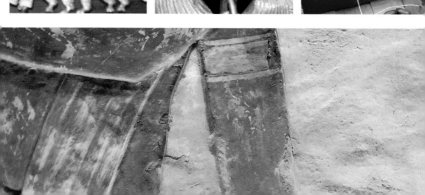

WALKS AND TOURS

DOWNTOWN CAIRO

Combining three of Egypt's top highlights – the Egyptian Museum, the Khan Al Khalili Bazaar and a felucca trip on the Nile – this full-day tour also gives a taste of the city with a stroll around the downtown area and Old Cairo, via some of its historic cafés.

DISTANCE 5.5km (3½ miles)
TIME A full day
START Egyptian Museum
END Khan Al Khalili Bazaar
POINTS TO NOTE
Count on at least 2–3 hours at the Egyptian Museum for the highlights alone (guides can do a tour in 1–1½hrs). Though always busy (particularly in winter), the museum is often quieter between 9am–10am, at lunchtime and late in the afternoon.

Buying a Guide
On the left, as you enter the Egyptian Museum, is the museum bookshop. It stocks an excellent selection of guides in various languages, though they are cheaper bought elsewhere *(see American University, p.38)*.

With its long and colourful history, Cairo is a fascinating place to explore. It's also one of the most vibrant cities in the world. Many visitors hurry in and hurry out, but a day or two spent discovering the capital dubbed 'Umm Ad Dunya' (the mother of the world) by its denizens is recommended.

EGYPTIAN MUSEUM

Liberation Square is home to the greatest collection of Ancient Egyptian artefacts in the world, the acclaimed **Egyptian Museum ❶**

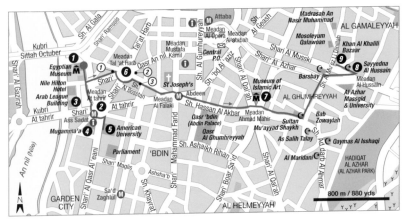

(Meadan At Tahrir; tel: 02-575 4319; www.egyptianmuseum.gov.eg; daily 8.30am–6.30pm; charge).

Though the museum is showing its age, a visit here remains one of the highlights of a trip to Egypt. It also serves as an ideal introduction to the ancient attractions of the Nile.

History

Purpose-built in 1902, the pink neo-classical museum was designed to house the collection begun by French archaeologist Auguste Mariette in the mid-1850s.

A brand-new, state-of the-art museum, named the Grand Egyptian Museum (www.gem.gov.eg), has finally commenced construction on the Giza Plateau. Costing over £320 million, it will house, among other things, the collection's masterpieces, but is not billed to open before 2014.

Collection

Since the museum contains more than a quarter of a million objects spanning over three millennia from the Old Kingdom to the Roman period, it would take at least nine months to see everything, and only if allowing a minute or less at each exhibit. That calculation doesn't include the vast number of artefacts languishing in the museum's basement. Some of the larger statues have reputedly sunk through the floor, earning the museum the ironic title of 'Egypt's last major excavation'. Cataloguing is now, however, under way.

Visiting and Guides

The ground floor is generally arranged chronologically (clockwise from the entrance hall), while exhibits on the first floor are grouped

Above from far left: golden mask of Tutankhamun in the Egyptian Museum; admiring the mummies.

Museum Highlights

The following lists the museum's top 20 highlights, as selected for this book by Professor Dr Zahi Hawass, Secretary General of Egypt's Supreme Council of Antiquities. GF = Ground Floor; UF = Upper Floor.

- Colossal statue of Akhenaten (GF room 3)
- Statue of Rameses II as a child with the Levantine sun-god Hauron (GF room 10)
- Bust of Thutmose III (GF room 12)
- Statue of Meritamun II (GF room 15)
- Copper statue of Pepy I or his son Merenra (GF room 31)
- Statuette of dwarf Seneb and his family (GF room 32)
- Four statues of Intyshedu (GF room 32)
- Sheikh el-Balad (GF room 42)
- Statue of Khafra (GF room 42)
- Statue of the dwarf Perniankhu (GF room 42)
- Narmer Palette (GF room 43)
- Statue of Kai (GF room 46)
- Three triads of Menkaura (GF room 47)
- Statue of Djoser (GF room 48)
- Golden mask of Psusennes I (UF room 2)
- Golden mask of Tutankhamun (UF room 3)
- Portrait of two brothers from the Fayoum (UF room 14)
- Golden throne of Tutankhamun (UF room 35)
- Innermost coffin of Yuya (UF room 43)
- Mummy of Hatshepsut (UF room 56)

Above from far left: outside the Egyptian Museum; Cairo's Meadan At Tahrir; Patisserie Groppi.

thematically. Tutankhamun's famous rooms are located on the first floor, as are the royal mummies and jewellery rooms. *For more on Tutankhamun's treasures, see box, p.72.*

The museum is ideally visited twice: once with a guide to point out the highlights (all contained in the main halls), and a second time alone wandering some of the side rooms, which give fascinating glimpses into the daily lives of the Ancient Egyptians. If you don't want a guide (LE50 per hour is the official rate; guiding standards are variable), it's easy to spot the highlights from the crowds of people around them. Alternatively, see our list of highlights in the box on p.37.

Tomb of Auguste Mariette

Before you leave the museum, check out the **tomb** of the French Egyptologist Auguste Mariette (1821–81; *see p.42*), in the eastern end of the garden. Above him are the busts of eminent Egyptologists including a rather grumpy-looking Champollion, who used the Rosetta Stone (a copy of London's original is found in the museum, diagonally opposite the entrance; it is the museum's only non-original artefact) to decipher hieroglyphs for the first time.

MEADAN AT TAHRIR

Next head out for **Meadan At Tahrir** ❷ (Liberation Square), Cairo's piv-

otal point. Its choked arteries sum up supremely the city's congestion problems. Dominating the skyline to the southwest is the **Nile Hilton**. Ugly 1950s-style it may be, but it was Cairo's first upmarket hotel and marks the site of a British army camp that once occupied much of the square.

Due south of the Hilton is the **Arab League Building** ❸, founded in Cairo in 1946 to 'consider in a general way the affairs and interests of Arab countries'. Representatives from the 22 member countries regularly meet here.

Further south is the **Mugamma'a** ❹, Egypt's Home Office, which employs around 18,000 civil servants. Bleak and vast, it was inspired and funded by the Soviets during Egypt's socialist dalliance.

American University

Across from Shari' Al Qasr Al 'eani is the more elegant Moorish-style complex of the **American University** ❺, where the country's elite receives an American education. Though the students have recently relocated to a campus to the east, the outstanding **AUC Bookshop** (at Ashaikh Rihan and Shari' Muhammad Mahmoud; tel: 02-2797 5929; Sat–Thur 10am–8pm, Fri 2–8pm) remains the best bookshop in Cairo and has several city branches and outlets. There's also a small café (daily 10am–5pm) and changing exhibitions.

Meadan and Shari 'Tal'at Harb

Retrace your steps, then turn right diagonally opposite the Egyptian Museum along Shari' Qasr An Nil to **Meadan Tal'at Harb** ❻. Khedive Ismail, Muhammad Ali's successor, was keen to establish Cairo's credentials on the international stage. He entertained grand plans for downtown Cairo in the 1860s after those for Paris, and even consulted that city's architect, Baron Haussmann. The square's main thoroughfares, Shari' Qasr An Nil and Shari' Tal'at Harb, used to be lined with trees and pavement cafés until the 1950s and '60s .

The two streets cross in the small, round square of Meadan Tal'at Harb, where **Patisserie Groppi**, see ⑪①, is found; this was the scene of elegant tea dances and de rigueur parties in the heady, pre-revolutionary days, when Cairo was known as 'Paris on the Nile'.

Leaving the square by turning right past the Air France office, Shari' Tal'at Harb passes **Café Riche**, see ⑪②, where Nasser's revolutionaries *(see p.33)* are said to have plotted the overthrow of King Farouk in 1952. Turn left into Shari' Hoda Shaarawi if you feel like lunch at **Felfella**, see ⑪③.

MUSEUM OF ISLAMIC ART

After lunch, take a taxi to Shari' Boar Sa'id near Bab Al Khalq (Al Khalq Gate) for the **Museum of Islamic Art**

❼ (Mathaf Al Islami; at Shari' Boar Sa'id and Shari' Al Qal'ah; tel: 02-2390 1520; daily 9am–5pm; charge), which lies approximately 1.7km (1 mile) east of Meadan At Tahrir.

The collection, dating from the 1880s, was mostly salvaged from mosques, *madrasahs* and palaces in Cairo's Old City, and is considered one of Islamic art's finest. Exhibits are well presented, date from the 7th to 18th centuries and range from exquisitely designed swords and functioning fountains to intricate *mashrabia* (wooden latticework), chandeliers and a carpet.

Occupying the upper floor is the **Library of Egypt** with its collection of 750,000 books and valuable manuscripts dating back to the 8th century.

Food and Drink

① PATISSERIE GROPPI
Meadan Tal'at Harb; tel: 02-391 1946; daily 7am–11pm; £
Only traces of the Art Deco style remain, but this is still an interesting stop for coffee and a cake after the museum.

② CAFÉ RICHE
17 Shari' Tal'at Harb; tel: 02-392 9793; daily 10am–midnight; £
Dating from 1908, this Cairo institution has been visited by many of the city's greatest thinkers and writers. Bustling and atmospheric, it's great for breakfast, and also serves alcohol.

③ FELFELLA RESTAURANT
Shari' Hoda Shaarawi, just off Shari' Tal'at Harb; tel: 02-392 2751; daily 7am–midnight; £–££
The family-run Felfella offers traditional Egyptian and Levantine cooking in pleasant surroundings. Though catering mainly to tourists, the food is decent. The *ta'amiyya* (deep-fried patties of fava beans) and stuffed pigeon are specialities.

Above from left:
Meadan Tal'at Harb
(see p.39); the pyra-
mids of Giza.

Khan Al Khalili
Founded in 1382
by Emir Al Khalil, a
Mamluk Master of the
Horse, Khan Al Khalili
quickly attracted both
local and foreign
traders including
Jews, Armenians and
Persians and began
to burgeon. With its
labyrinth of streets
and alleyways, it's
also seen its fair share
of iniquity over the
years, and has also
provided a handy
refuge for dissident
groups, which has led
to its frequent raiding
by the authorities.

OLD CAIRO

Take a taxi *(see route on map)* from
the museum to **Meadan Al Hussain**,
or walk back along Shari' Boar Sai'd,
taking a right along the busy Shari'
Al Azhar, until you arrive on the
square. Use the underpass to reach
the **Mosque of Sayyedna Al Hussain** ❽ (closed to non-Muslims),
believed to house the head of Hussain,
the Prophet Muhammad's grandson,
and one of the holiest Shi'ite sites in
Egypt. The building itself dates to the
late 19th century.

Khan Al Khalili Bazaar

As you face the mosque, take the
alley that leads left into the **Khan Al
Khalili Bazaar** ❾ (Mon–Sat 9am–
6pm or later). Known locally as 'The
Khan', Khan Al Khalili has served as
Cairo's main market for some 700
years. Though the market has been
on the tourist trail for centuries, locals
still come here to shop, particularly
for gold, fabrics, perfume and spices.

Nonetheless, it's well worth escaping
the main thoroughfares and roaming
at random among the alleyways.
You'll soon find Naguib Mahfouz's
Midaq Alley, so vividly described in
his novel of the same name. If you get
lost (which is to be recommended),
simply ask for Jami' Al Hussain (Al
Hussain Mosque).

For a post-shopping pit-stop, head
down the first alley to the left of Al
Hussain after passing a few cafés to
Al Fishawi café *(see p.49)*. For a more
substantial meal, head for **Café Naguib
Mahfouz** *(see p.49)*; return to the
bazaar's main alley, Shari' Al Badestane,
which runs from the Mosque of Al
Hussain to the Gold Bazaar *(see p.49)*
on Shari' Al Mu'ez Li Dinillah; the restaurant is halfway along the street.

NILE FELUCCA TRIP

If time allows, a trip on the Nile on a
felucca (the wooden sailboats used on
the Nile for centuries) is a good addition to this tour. Return to Meadan Al
Hussain and take a taxi from Shari' Al
Azhar to the Nile, opposite the Four
Seasons Nile Plaza Hotel, where you
can hire a felucca for LE40–50 per
hour (for the boat, which usually seats
up to 10 passengers; tip the captain
afterwards). Then, like the Ancient
Egyptians, you can watch the sun's
dying in the west.

Butterflies of the Nile

Dancing across the Nile's surface like butterflies or baller-
inas, feluccas form one of the Nile's most beautiful sights.
Unmistakable for their white lateen (triangular sail), they
also have very shallow draughts, which allow them to
navigate shallow waters, and to be rowed when the wind
drops. Sometimes they're still used for their traditional
purpose of transporting cargo, including crops and animals, up and down the Nile; today, of course, they are
also used for tourism.

THE PYRAMIDS AND THE SPHINX

Egypt's pyramids are the oldest of the major pharaonic sites and, along with the enigmatic Sphinx, also their most iconic. This full-day tour takes in all the major monuments and ends with the perfect panoramic photo opportunity.

The sole-surviving Wonder of the Ancient World, the pyramids of Giza must be the oldest and most-visited tourist attraction in history. En route from Cairo, a stop-off at the ancient capital of Memphis is recommended, as is a visit to the necropolis of Saqarah, where the extraordinary tradition of pyramid-building first began.

MEMPHIS

Start the tour at **Memphis ❶** (daily 8am–4pm, summer to 5pm; charge), located 25km (15½ miles) south of Cairo, near the modern-day village of Mit Rahinah. Though there's scant evidence of it today, Memphis was the world's first imperial city, fabled for its magnificent monuments, palaces and landscaped gardens. Founded around 3100 BC by King Menes (Narmer) on the spot where the delta met the southern Nile Valley, it symbolised physically and metaphorically the newly unified Egypt. Memphis grew to become a highly prosperous commercial hub, an important cult centre for the god

DISTANCE 180km (110 miles)
TIME A full day
START Memphis
END Pyramid of Menkaura
POINTS TO NOTE
As there is no public transport between sites (distances are quite far), you'll need to take a taxi. The cheapest, quickest option is to hire a taxi for the day (LE250–350), or take an organised tour.

Be Prepared
The heat in the desert and pyramid tombs can be ferocious. Wear light clothes, a hat, good shoes (particularly if planning to visit the tombs), and bring plenty of water and sun cream. There are limited restaurant options, so you may want to bring a picnic.

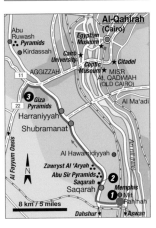

Memphis Sphinx
Just beyond the museum at Memphis *(see right)*, look out for the beautiful alabaster sphinx thought to date from the New Kingdom. Measuring 8m (26ft) by 4m (13ft), it is the second-largest surviving Sphinx in Egypt (after its much more famous cousin in Giza).

Still Searching
The French Egyptologist Auguste Mariette *(see p.38)* uncovered many of Saqarah's sites in the 1850s. Discoveries continue today; of recent major interest was the unearthing of the mummified remains of a royal scribe and butler in 2007. Two-thirds of Saqarah remains unexcavated.

Ptah and served as Egypt's capital for over 1,500 years.

Although the grandeur is long gone – eroded by weather, pillaged by invaders and buried by the Nile's annual flooding – there are some interesting vestiges to be found in the **museum** (daily 9am–6pm, summer to 6.30pm; charge), including a beautifully carved fallen colossus of Rameses II as a young man.

SAQARAH

From Mit Rahinah, drive past fields and lush palm groves to the ticket office for the complex of nearby **Saqarah ❷** (daily 8am–4pm, summer to 5pm; charge for North Saqarah, plus separate charges for various tombs). At the car park, give your driver an idea of how long you will spend on the site (2–2½ hours should be sufficient).

Saqarah was the favoured burial site of the Old Kingdom pharaohs and was used for the interment of prominent members of society for more than 3,500 years. It is still one of Egypt's largest cemeteries and the country's most extensive archaeological site, encompassing no fewer than 11 pyramids and several hundred tombs and mastabas, including those of sacred animals.

Step Pyramid of King Djoser
Walk up the path towards the original, but restored 1.6km (1-mile) long limestone enclosure wall. A covered pillared corridor, the hypostyle hall, leads to the Great Court of the complex of the **Step Pyramid of King Djoser Ⓐ**.

Before its construction, Egyptian notables were buried in mud-brick mastabas *(see p29)*. When King Djoser, in the 27th century BC, decided he wanted something more long-lasting, his Chief Architect, Imhotep, had the genius to place mastabas one on top of the other, and to opt for stone over mud brick. By doing so he created the world's first stone-build pyramid, which with its original gleaming limestone casing once towered 62m (203ft) high, and 118m (387ft) by 140m (460ft) around the base.

A 28m (95ft) deep shaft leads into the burial chamber, but the latter is now closed to the public to protect it. To the right of the courtyard is the **Heb Sed Court**, where every seven

years a festival was held in which the king symbolically renewed his vitality.

Beyond are the **Houses of the South and the North**, probably older shrines representing Upper and Lower Egypt and, at the back, the **Serdab**, with a copy of Djoser's statue.

Pyramids of Unas and Teti

Southwest of the Great Court is a deep shaft where the king's viscera are thought to have been buried in canopic jars. Just behind the shaft, walk south along the western edge and then down to the Causeway of Unas, before walking back along it towards the **Pyramid of Unas** ❸ (2374–2350 BC; currently closed to the public), built 300 years after the Step Pyramid.

Though little more than a large pile of rubble today, the structure once reached nearly 45m (148ft) in height. Inside, the walls of the burial chamber are covered with the so-called Pyramid Texts, the earliest known decorative writing found in a tomb. It marked the start of the tradition of pharaonic tomb painting *(see p.31)*.

Drive northeast of the Step Pyramid for the **Pyramid of Teti** ❹, who ruled from 2340–2325 BC. Pillaged of both its tomb treasures and its limestone casing, little of this step pyramid remains. Inside the decorated burial chamber, look out for the hieroglyphic inscriptions on the sarcophagus, the first of its kind.

Mastabas and Serapeum

Nearby are the 6th-Dynasty (2345–2181 BC) mastabas of the viziers Mereruka, Ankh-Mahor and Kagemni, among the largest and most finely decorated Old Kingdom nobles' tombs. The decorations include domestic scenes, hunting, sport-playing and farming.

Two hundred metres/yds further on is the impressive double **Mastaba of Akhet-Hotep and Ptah-Hotep**, a priest and his son, who both served as viziers. Here you can see the different stages of tomb decoration as well as some beautifully executed reliefs.

One of the most impressive and fascinating monuments is the **Serapeum** (currently closed to the public). A vast, rock-cut subterranean gallery, it served as the burial place for the mummified sacred Apis bulls that were worshipped as an incarnation of the god Ptah, patron of Memphis.

On the other side of the Serapeum is the 5th-century BC **Mastaba of Ti**, the royal hairdresser and overseer of the pyramids and temples. It is considered the most elaborate and artistically accomplished of the Saqarah nobles' tombs and contains some of the most vibrant scenes of daily life. Look out for the hieroglyphs, which issue from the scenes like cartoon speech balloons.

Nearby, a small stall sells soft drinks. For a picnic, local families head to the shade of the ruins of the 5th-century **Coptic Monastery of St Jeremiah** (destroyed by Arab invaders

Above from far left: taking a break from sightseeing; there are no fewer than 11 pyramids at Saqarah, including the Step Pyramid of King Djoser; to avoid the crowds, it's best to come early in the morning or late in the afternoon.

Who Built the Pyramids?

According to recent research – and contrary to popular Hollywood-fed misconceptions – the pyramids were not believed to have been built by slave labour brutally enforced, but by local farmers in need of work and a wage during the flood season, when the Nile submerged their fields. The higher water level also aided the transportation of the giant building blocks *(see margin, p.28)*. On the vast building sites were lodgings, kitchens and even medical clinics.

Above from left:
the pyramids of Giza
and the Sphinx.

Ticket Tip
Sales of pyramid
tomb tickets are
limited to 300 a day:
150 go on sale at
7.30am, 150 at 1pm,
so arrive early.
Visitors are no longer
allowed to climb any
of the pyramids, or
take photographs
inside the tombs.

in the 10th century), just south of the
Causeway of Unas. Otherwise drive
along the canal towards Giza, and
have lunch at **Andrea**, see ⑪①, or
Felafala, see ⑪②.

PYRAMIDS OF GIZA AND THE SPHINX

Drive to the pyramids' ticket office
(daily 7.30am–4pm; charge – cash
only, separate charges for the Solar
Barque Museum and two of the
three tombs of the pyramids – Khufu,
Khafra and Menkaura – which open
by rotation).

The sole surviving Wonder of the
Ancient World, Egypt's **pyramids of
Giza ❸** remain as impressive to visitors
today as they must have been 46 centuries ago, when they were first built.

Great Pyramid of Khufu

The oldest and largest of the three pyramids is the **Great Pyramid of Khufu
Ⓐ** (Cheops; *c.* 2547–*c.*2524 BC), built
with no fewer than 2.3 million blocks
weighing between 2.5 and 15 tonnes
each. With the original limestone casing
(requisitioned for other buildings over
the succeeding centuries), the pyramid
towered 146.6m (480ft) high. Three
chambers were found inside; all were
empty except for Khufu's sarcophagus.

Entering this pyramid is not for the
claustrophobic, elderly or very unfit,
as the corridor is low and narrow, and
it often lacks air. The corridor leads
via the **Queen's Chamber** into the
spectacular 47m (154ft) long **Great
Gallery**, which ends at the **King's
Chamber** with its pillaged and now
empty sarcophagus.

The Great Pyramid
Giza's Great Pyramid
took around 20 years
to complete, which
would have required
the laying of nearly 12
blocks an hour, even
working 24 hours a
day. The entrance to
the Great Pyramid,
carefully disguised by
using a block identical
to the others,
remained a secret for
over three millennia.

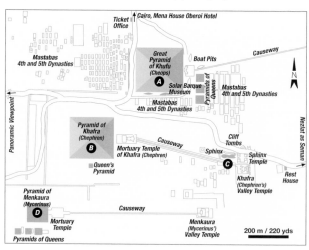

At the back of the pyramid is the **Solar Barque Museum** (charge), which showcases an extraordinary 43m (141ft) long boat. An interesting exhibition documents the excavation.

Here, also, are three smaller **Queens' Pyramids** and the ruins of the king's funerary temple.

Pyramid of Khafra

Better preserved is the whole complex around the **Pyramid of Khafra ⓑ** (Chephren; *c*.2516–*c*.2493 BC), Khufu's son, which lies southwest of his pyramid. Khafra's pyramid appears taller, but is actually built on higher ground and is slightly smaller, at 136m (447ft). Unusually, the apex is still covered by the original limestone casing. The pyramid has two chambers, one of which contains the king's sarcophagus.

The Sphinx

Walk eastwards down the road to the remains of **Khafra's Mortuary Temple** and of the **Causeway** leading to his **Valley Temple** that is guarded by the ever-enigmatic **Sphinx ⓒ**. Though the face appears to resemble that of Khafra, the monument is believed to pre-date the rest of the Khafra complex by over 2,600 years. The Sphinx has suffered over the ages: its nose was chiselled off sometime between the 10th and 15th centuries, and part of the fallen beard now resides in the British Museum in London. Named by the Greeks after the mythical half-woman, half-lion monster of ancient times, the origin, purpose and date of the Sphinx remains unknown. Carved from bedrock, it has stood the test of time thanks largely to it being covered over the centuries by sand.

Pyramid of Menkaura

Back on the plateau the smaller, third **Pyramid of Menkaura ⓓ** (Mycerinus; 2532–2504 BC), built by Khafra's son, is surrounded by a couple of ruined temples also built for Menkaura. From here, the road leads to a panoramic plateau for the glorious view of all three pyramids. Then perhaps visit **Mena House Oberoi**, see ⑪③, before heading back to town.

Shows at the Sphinx

The Giza Sound and Light show is held nightly in front of the Sphinx (tel: 02-3385 2880; www.soundandlight. com.eg; times vary).

Horse/Camel Trips

If you fancy galloping a horse or trotting a camel around the pyramids at dusk, the reputable AA Stable (Shari' Abu Al Hood, Giza; tel: 02-3385 0531; daily 7am–8pm) costs LE40/50/ 120 per hour for horse/ camel/carriage) rides.

Food and Drink 🍴

① ANDREA

59 Tir'at Al Maryutiya, Giza (north of Pyramid Road on Al Maryutiya Canal); tel: 02-3383 1133; daily 10am–midnight; ££

Dine on a chicken spit-roast or excellent *mezze*, salads and quail in a verdant garden full of shade and birdsong and, at weekends, chattering middle-class Egyptian families.

② FELAFELA

27 Cairo Alexandria Road; tel: 02-3376 1234; daily 9am–midnight; £

Between Saqarah and Giza, the Felafela enjoys a fanatical local following for its excellent traditional food at great prices. Takeaway is available too if you want to grab something for a picnic.

③ MENA HOUSE OBEROI

Near the Giza pyramids; Shari' Al Ahram; tel: 02-3377 3222; www.menahouseoberoi.com; £££–££££

Set at the foot of the pyramids, the Mena has unbeatable views. Its range of bars and restaurants serve everything from cocktails to a light lunch or five-course dinner.

MEDIEVAL CAIRO

With over 850 listed monuments packed into a few square kilometres, medieval Cairo is one of the most heritage-rich enclaves in the world. For many, it is Cairo's most fascinating quarter and a world away from the modern downtown area.

DISTANCE 2km (1¼ miles)
TIME A busy half-day
START Bab Zowaylah
END Bab Al Futuh
POINTS TO NOTE
Modest dress isn't just polite, it's essential if you want to enter mosques. Shoes should be left at the mosque door; sometimes shoe coverings are provided. Shoe attendants, and any guardian who opens a door to anything, will expect tips, so bring lots of change. Avoid Fridays, when the mosques close for prayer (between 11am–1.30pm). If you find a monument closed (the less-visited ones sometimes are), hunt around for the guardian, who's normally close by.

Sultan Al Hakim
One of Egypt's most notorious rulers was the sixth Fatimid sultan, Al Hakim, and many stories surround his reign. It is said that he changed the working day to night because he couldn't stand daylight; that he loathed women so much that he ordered the closure of all factories fabricating women's shoes, and that he had swindling merchants sodomised by his Nubian slave. Murdering at random those who displeased him, the sultan himself met a premature end in mysterious circumstances.

This walking tour, centred on medieval Cairo's principal thoroughfare, Shari' Al Mu'ez Li Dinillah, will take you back in time. Like market-goers for millennia, you still need to dodge the donkey-carts clattering down the alleyways. In the souqs, the smell of pungent spices and cooking food still tickles your nose, and the cries and banter of the *gallabiyya*-clad vendors still assail your ears.

Extending from the old gate of Bab Zowaylah in the south to Bab Al Futuh in the north, Al Qahirah, as it's known in Arabic, is as well preserved atmospherically as it is architecturally, and is quite simply one of the finest medieval cities in the world.

BAB ZOWAYLAH AND AROUND

Lying just outside the Bab Zowaylah is the large, rectangular 12th-century Fatimid **Mosque of Salih Talay** (currently closed for restoration).

Stretching out from just in front of the mosque is the cloth-covered **Souq Al Khayyameyyah** (Tentmakers' Bazaar), which used to furnish the Fatimid armies with tents and saddles in the 11th century. Today, its workshops produce the tents Cairenes use at important social events, as well as wall hangings, carpets and cushion covers.

Directly opposite the bazaar stands the monumental 10th-century **Bab Zowaylah ❶** (Shari' Ahmad Mahir;

daily 8.30am–5pm; charge). It's one of the last remaining gates of the medieval city, and during Mamluk and Ottoman times public executions were held in front of it. The Bab houses a visitor centre with panels about the ancient gate's history.

Both the ramparts and the minarets (which belong to the adjacent 15th-century **Mosque-Madrasah of Sultan Mu'ayyad Shaykh**) are accessible from the gate and offer spectacular and unmatched views over the Old City. From the Bab's platform, Mamluk sultans would see off the annual *mahmal* (caravan of pilgrims) embarking on the long and dangerous journey to Mecca. The mosque itself is worth a peek for its 15th-century cedarwood and gold-leaf ceiling, ebony and ivory-inlaid *minbar* (pulpit) and heavy bronze doors.

Continue along Shari' Al Mu'ez Li Dinillah. Look out for the **cotton merchants** selling sacks of raw cotton as they have done for centuries, and the **ice-block sellers** with their donkeys. Around 100m/yds further to the left lie Cairo's last remaining **fez shops**, selling headgear worn today largely by Egypt's older generation.

GHURIYA

Just before the intersection with Shari' Al Azhar is the splendid 16th-century **Al Ghuri complex** ❷ (Shari' Al Mu'ez Li Dinillah; daily 9am–6pm;

free) built by Cairo's last Mamluk sultan, Al Ghuri. Here, to the left is the **Mosque-Madrasah (Massgid wa Madrasah) of Al Ghuri** with its tall, square, red minaret and intricately decorated interior; across the street

[Map]

AL HUSAYNEYYAH
Darb As Sammakin
Shari' Al Husariya
BAB AN NASSR CEMETERY
Shari' Al Baghghalah
Bab Al Futuh ❻
Bab An Nassr
❺
Al Hakim
Old City Wall
Ousun Wikala
Bayt As Sehaimi
Sabil-Kuttub Sulayman Agha Al Silahdar
❹
AL GAMALEYYAH
Shari' Al Gamaleyyah
Al Aqmar
Monastery of Baibars II
Sabil-Kuttub Abd Ar Rahman Katkhudah
Qasr Bashtak
Palace of Musafirk-hanah
Madrasah wa Khanqah Barquq
Egyptian Textile Museum
Madrasah An Nasir Muhammad
❹
Madrasah-Mosoleum Qalawoan
As Salih Najm Addin Mausoleum
Sayyedna Al Hussain
Khan Al Khalili Bazaar
❸ ❷
Meadan Al Hussain
Gold Bazaar
Shari' Goahar Al Qa'id
Souq Al'attarin
Shari' Al Azhar
Madrasah Sultan Al Ashraf Bersby
Meadan Al Azhar
① Al Azhar
❷
❸
Massgid wa Madrasah Al Ghuri
Al Ghuri Mausoleum
Wikala Al Ghuri
Souq Al Harireyyin (Silk-Merchants' Bazaar)
★ Fez Shops
AL GUMHUREYYAH
★ Fakahani
Sultan Mu'ayyad Shaykh
AD DARB AL AHMAR
Bab Zowaylah
Shari' Ahmad Mahir
As Salih Talay
Souq Al Khayyameyyah (Tentmakers' Bazaar)
Ahmad Mihmandar
Al Maridani ★
200 m / 220 yds

Useful References
For more information on Cairo's remarkable Islamic monuments, check out the website www.cim.gov.eg. Various books published by the AUC Press and available in Cairo (www.auc.com) also cover the subject comprehensively, including *A Walk Through the Islamic City* by Jim Antoniou, and *Islamic Monuments in Cairo: The Practical Guide* by Caroline Williams, both of which should be available in the AUC Bookshop (see p.38).

is his **Mausoleum and Sabil-Kuttub** (Fountain and Qur'anic School).

Turn right and walk east through the fabric stalls for around 150m/yds to the **Wikala Al Ghuri** (tel: 02-2511 0472; admission for shows), a carefully restored caravanserai *(see below)* now housing craft shops and artists' workshops and hosting regular nightly performances of Sufi dancing *(see p.122)*.

Above: details of the Mosque of Al Azhar.

MOSQUE AND MADRASAH OF AL AZHAR

Continuing along the street you come to one of Cairo's oldest mosques and certainly its most distinguished: the **Mosque of Al Azhar** ❸ ('the Blooming'; daily 9am–5pm; free). Built in AD 971, it was the Fatimids' first, and formed the heart and soul of their new city. Its **madrasah**, the oldest

educational institution in the world after the Kairaouine in Fez, Morocco, was world famous as a centre of Sunni learning. It still is, and its Sheikh remains Egypt's supreme Muslim theological authority and is entitled to issue fatwas (public condemnations).

Enter the mosque through the lovely 15th-century **Barber's Gate**, where students traditionally had their heads shaved. On both sides of the entrance lies the 14th-century madrasah. The part on the right contains Al Azhar's most precious and oldest manuscripts.

Overlooking the 10th-century courtyard are three minarets, reflecting in their different styles their different dates (14th–16th centuries).

Behind the mosque are **modern university buildings** accommodating the students who still travel here to study from all across the Muslim world – look out for them quietly studying

Caravanserais

The remains of over 30 *wikalas* (caravanserais or merchant inns) can be found in Cairo's medieval city, particularly in the Al Gamaleyyah area (named after the street which runs south of the Mosque of Al Hakim). In medieval times, though, nearly 400 *wikalas* were found here. These caravanserais generally followed a set plan throughout the Islamic world: stables, shops, a kitchen and storehouses for merchandise were built around a central courtyard on the ground floor, while simple rooms for the merchants were located on the upper floors. Guarded, stout entrance doors kept the *wikala*'s occupants and their valuable goods safe from robbers at night.

the holy scriptures in the shadow of the arcades.

For a quick coffee or a soothing *sheesha*, head straight for **Suliman Café**, see ⑪①, by the side of the mosque. Opposite is a popular traditional herbalist, **Ahmed Zalat** (daily 9am–midnight).

Walk back to the Al Ghuri complex and use the pedestrian bridge to continue along Shari' Al Mu'ez Li Dinillah. If you feel like more refreshments or something to eat, take the underpass to Meaden Al Hussain to seek out the famous **Al Fishawi** café, see ⑪②, or the slightly smarter **Café Naguib Mahfouz**, see ⑪③, before returning along Shari' Al Azhar to the foot of the pedestrian bridge.

Back on Shari' Al Mu'ez Li Dinillah, the imposing 15th-century **Madrasah of Sultan Al Ashraf Bersby** is worth popping into for its celestial dome, fine *minbar* (pulpit) made with cedarwood and ivory inlay work, and marble paving. The first alley to the left before the madrasah leads into the **Perfume and Spice Bazaar**, where pungent *filfil* (black pepper), *kamum* (cumin), *shatta* (chilli) and *karkadeh* (hibiscus flower) all make great local buys.

BETWEEN TWO PALACES

Return to Shari' Al Mu'ez Li Dinillah and cross over Shari' Al Muski, bustling with market-goers, to the glittering **Gold Bazaar**. Small pas-

sageways to the right lead into **Khan Al Khalili** *(see margin, p.40).*

After 150m/yds, the street turns into Shari' An Nahaseen (Coppersmiths' Street), with, on the right side, the 13th-century **Mausoleum of As Salih Najm Addin**, Cairo's very first Qur'anic school.

This area is known as Bayn Al Qasrayn, 'Between the Two Palaces', after the great Fatimid palaces that used to dominate the quarter, marking the heart of their capital.

Above from far left: devotees at the Mosque of Al Azhar; ceiling of the Madrasah and Khanqah of Barquq *(see p.50)*; Al Fishawi.

Food and Drink

① SULIMAN CAFÉ
Shari' Sheikh Muhammad Abdouh, next to Al Azhar Mosque; daily 7am–midnight
A traditional and much-loved Cairene 'ahwa (coffee shop), Suliman is laid-back, liberal (women are welcome) and peaceful. With tables spilling into the souq, it's a prime place for people-watching. If you fancy trying a *sheesha*, here's the place. Food isn't served.

② AL FISHAWI
Off Meaden Al Hussain; tel: 02-590 6755; daily 24hrs
Dating back to 1771, Al Fishawi is an institution. Though much frequented now by tourists and expats, the café retains a loyal Cairene following, and is still a popular meeting place for well-heeled artists and intellectuals. Buzzing and atmospheric, it's famous for its coffee and mint tea. Food isn't served.

③ CAFÉ NAGUIB MAHFOUZ
5 Sikket Al Baddistan, Khan Al Khalili; tel: 02-590 3788; daily 10am–2am; ££
Though also patronised by Cairo's artists (including the late Naguib Mahfouz, the café's namesake), the atmosphere's very different to Al Fishawi: with its marble floors, uniformed waiters and air-con, it's cool, serene and somewhat smart. *Sheesha*-smoking is popular. Snacks are served, and an upmarket restaurant adjoins.

Above: street surveillance; Souq Al Khayyameyyah (Tentmakers' Bazaar; *see p.46*).

Later rulers replaced the palaces with their own monuments, and here, where the street opens up, on its western side, are three monumental, contiguous **Mamluk complexes** (Shari' Al Mu'ez Li Dinillah; daily 8am–5pm; charge for each monument). Nowhere in the world does such a short stretch of street contain so many madrasahs, mausoleums and *khanqahs* (Sufi 'monasteries').

Madrasahs, Mausoleums and More

First in the complex on the left is its oldest building and its highlight: the well-restored **Madrasah and Mausoleum (Mosoleyum) of Qalawoan**, built in 1279. The mausoleum is beautifully decorated with inlaid stones, painted stucco, cedarwood, *zellij* (tilework) and stained glass.

Also in the complex is the unmarked **Maristan of Sultan Qalawoan**, a medieval hospital that continued in use as a medical centre right until the 19th century. Its inspiration was a *maristan* in medieval Damascus that so impressed Qalawoan that he decided to create his own in Cairo.

The **Madrasah and Dome of Sultan An Nasir Muhammad ❹**, Qalawoan's son, stands next door. Built in 1304, it is a hotchpotch of architectural styles, including an incongruous-looking marble Gothic doorway pilfered from a church in Palestine after the routing of the Crusaders by the sultan in 1291.

Next door is the **Madrasah and Khanqah of Barquq**, built in 1304 and identifiable for its distinct black-and-white marble portal, and impressive bronze doors. It contains the very ornate domed tomb of his daughter. The covered court to the right of the entrance passageway contains four recycled pharaonic columns made of porphyry. Opposite, the new **Egyptian Textile Museum** should soon open.

Palaces, Fountains and Mosques

Around 50m/yds down from Barquq's complex are the two remaining floors (of five original ones) of the 14th-century **Palace (Qasr) of Bashtak**, a wonderful example of medieval secular architecture. Diagonally opposite is the elegant and much-photographed **Sabil-Kuttub of Abd Ar Rahman Katkhudah**, built in 1744 by an apparently dissolute emir as atonement for his sins. Sabil were public fountains; look for the remains of the fountain, and above it, the Qur'anic school.

Take the left street at this fork, proceeding past metalware shops to the **Mosque of Al Aqmar**, 'the Moonlit', built in 1125. It has beautiful *muqarnas* (stalactite-like decorative vaulting) on its ornate facade and is Cairo's earliest example of Fatimid architecture.

One block further along, turn right into the heavily renovated alley of **Darb Al Asfar** for an idea of the government's vision for medieval Cairo.

The finest house here is the labyrinthine-like **Bayt As Sehaimi** (daily 9am–5pm, summer to 6pm; charge), a former *wikala (see p.48)* dating from the 17th and 18th centuries. Try and find the bedroom with an early en-suite bathroom.

Returning to the main street you'll pass **Ghanim**, see ⑪④, a great spot for lunch. It's marked in Arabic only, but look for the wrought-iron fish beside the door. Back on the main street, on the corner, is the 1839-built **Mosque and Sabil-Kuttub of Sulayman Agha Al Silahdar**, its pencil-shaped minaret betraying the Ottoman influence during Muhammad Ali's reign.

MOSQUE OF AL HAKIM

Marking the final section of Shari' Al Mu'ez is the pungent onion and garlic market, with, at the far end, the **Mosque of Al Hakim** ❺ (daily 9am–5pm, free). Built between AD 990–1012, the mosque is one of Cairo's oldest, with the city's earliest minarets, and with marble floors and ablution fountain. Before its restoration in the 1980s by Ismaili Shi'ites, it served diverse functions, ranging from a Crusader prison to a sanitarium.

BAB AL FUTUH

Adjacent to the mosque is the monumental 11th-century **Bab Al Futuh** ❻ and **Fatimid walls**, which served along with Bab An Nassr as the two principal entrances to the Fatimid city. At Bab Al Futuh, crowds would gather to watch the returning *mahmal*, pilgrims who had successfully made the gruelling journey to and from Mecca.

The walls were originally built with stones reused from pharaonic structures in Memphis; in certain parts, tell-tale cartouches can be spotted. The great Muslim leader, Salah Addin (Saladin), reinforced the walls in the 12th century.

From Bab Al Futuh you can either walk back via Bab An Nassr and Shari' Al Gamaleyyah to Meaden Al Hussain (around 20 minutes) or, if flagging, hail one of the many taxis circulating near the Bab.

If you are here in the evening, you may want want to consider staying on for the Sufi show put on at the Wikala Al Ghuri *(see p.48)*.

Above from far left: ablution fountain and courtyard at the Mosque of Al Hakim; the sturdy 10th-century Bab Zowaylah *(see p.46)* gate.

Restoring Medieval Cairo

The Ministry of Culture has recently embarked on an ambitious and wholesale restoration project of medieval Cairo; so far 33 monuments have been restored.

Food and Drink 🍴

④ GHANIM

Darb Al Asfar, 30m/yds west of Bayt As Sehaimi; tel: 02-593 0586; Mon–Sat 10am–11pm; £
Much loved by locals and the quarter's best-kept secret is Ghanim. Fish and seafood, the speciality, are morning-fresh, artfully cooked and astonishingly good value. The interior, neo-Fatimid in keeping with the quarter, is small but cosy and very friendly. For fish, don't miss it.

ISLAMIC CAIRO AND THE CITADEL

Beginning with Cairo's early buildings, the tour is a walk through the city's history, taking in along the way some of the most important historical and religious buildings in both Cairo and the Islamic world. It ends with the city's most recent creation, the beautiful and restorative Al Azhar Park.

DISTANCE 5.5km (3¼ miles)
TIME A half-day
START Mosque of Ibn Tuloan
END Al Azhar Park
POINTS TO NOTE
This tour can be combined with the previous tour (Medieval Cairo, *see p.46*) or the following (Coptic Cairo, *see p.57*). For the former, you can either return from Al Azhar Park to Meadan Salah Addin and then on to Bab Zowaylah (about a 40-minute walk) or take a taxi. For Coptic Cairo, you'll need to take a taxi. Both men and women should be respectfully dressed; women will need a headscarf for some mosques (though this can usually be provided in those used to tourists).

A Case of Déjà Vu?
Something familiar about the Gayer-Anderson Museum? It's a favourite film set and featured in the James Bond film *The Spy Who Loved Me*.

Home to several famous mosques, this part of the city is known popularly as 'Islamic Cairo' – but it is very much more. For centuries the seat of Egypt's rulers, and a major outpost of many Islamic empires, the quarter has seen the unfolding of many major national and international events.

MOSQUE OF IBN TULOAN

Cairo's oldest-surviving intact mosque – and one of its largest and most impressive – is the **Mosque of Ibn Tuloan ❶** (Shari' As Salibah; daily 8am–6pm; free). It was built between 876–9 by Ahmed Ibn Tuloan, the Abbasid ruler, who, it is believed, based the design on the mosques of his homeland in modern-day Iraq. The spiral minaret in particular – a style previously unknown in Cairo – mirrors that of the Great Mosque of Samarra. The 'incense pot'-shaped filial adorning the top of the minaret is a later addition. The pointed arches of the double arcade surrounding the courtyard are the first to be used in any building in Cairo, and precede their discovery in Europe (in the Gothic style) by a quarter of a century.

Constructed of red brick and stucco, the mosque covers an area of more

than 3 hectares (7½ acres). Look out, along the back of the prayer hall, for the 2km (1¼-mile) long frieze that is beautifully carved with an inscription of the Qur'an in Kufic script.

To climb the **minaret** (free), follow the wall of the mosque to the left as you exit to reach it. From the top, there are stunning views over the mosque, Citadel and Old City all the way to Khan Al Khalili Bazaar and beyond.

GAYER-ANDERSON MUSEUM

A gateway 50m/yds to the right of the mosque as you exit leads to the **Gayer-Anderson Museum ❷** (Bayt Al Kiretleyyah; Shari' Ibn Tuloan; tel: 02-2364 7822; daily 9am–4pm; charge). The museum's namesake, the English major and army doctor John Gayer-Anderson, served as physician to the royal household from 1935–42,

and was an avid collector of oriental furniture, paintings and objets d'art. He also lovingly restored and joined together the two 16th-century buildings that house the collection, and 'themed' them in different oriental styles from Damascene and Moorish to Persian.

THE QASABA

Turn left from the museum to return to the main street, Shari' As Salibah,

Above from far left: Cairo's Citadel dominates the city skyline.

Above: Gayer-Anderson Museum; Mosque of Ibn Tuloan.

Souvenirs

Lying across the street from the entrance to the Mosque of Ibn Tuloan is Khan Mism Tuloan (Shari' As Salibah; tel: 02-2365 2227; daily 10am–5pm), a quality craft shop. Stuffed with arts and crafts from all across Egypt, it's the result of 30 years' collecting by the obliging French owner, Maryse.

and turn right. This street follows the **Qasaba ❸**, the main thoroughfare in medieval times, and lined with old palaces and mosques, many of them painstakingly restored following earthquake damage in the 1990s.

On the left, around 80m/yds up, look out for the 15th-century Mamluk **Mosque-Madrasah of Prince Taghri Bardi** and 50m/yds further on, the ornate 19th-century **Sabil-Kuttub of Umm Abbas** (public fountain; currently closed). Another 20m/yds further on and facing each other lie the 14th-century **Amir Shaykhu's Khanqah**, to the right, with a pharaonic cornice above the gate, and his **mosque**. Another 150m/yds further on the right is the **Sabil-Kuttub of Sultan Qayetbay** with a colourful facade.

MOSQUE-MADRASAH OF SULTAN HASSAN

Take the left street at the fork, past one of Cairo's bleakest prisons on the left, leading to Meadan Salah Addin.

At the time the citadel was built, this crossroads was the site of an arena used for horse races and Mamluk celebrations. Walk left towards the **Mosque-Madrasah of Sultan Hassan ❹** (Meadan Salah Addin; daily 8am–5pm, summer to 6pm; charge). The entrance is via a side door.

Built by Sultan Hassan between 1356 and 1363, the mosque-madrasah is Islam's largest medieval religious

Above: Mosque of Ar Rifa'i; Mosque of Muhammad Ali.

monument, Cairo's finest example of Mamluk architecture and a masterpiece of Islamic art.

Through the impressive entrance, a gloomy passageway leads to a dazzlingly bright central **courtyard** *(sahn)* crowned by a soaring dome.

Covering over 10,000 sq m (108,000 sq ft), the vast structure was built on a cruciform plan with four *liwans* (halls) branching off the central courtyard and serving as *madrasahs* (Islamic schools), each representing one of the four main schools of Sunni Islam.

In the eastern *liwan*, look out for the *mihrab* (niche indicating the direction of Mecca), exquisitely decorated with coloured marble. On the right, a bronze door decorated with silver and gold leads to the richly ornamented **Mausoleum of Hassan** surmounted by a dome that was restored by the Ottomans after its collapse during an earthquake in 1660. In the southeastern corner stands an elegant **minaret**, which, at nearly 82m (269ft), is Cairo's tallest.

MOSQUE OF AR RIFA'I

Across from Sultan Hassan's mosque lies the **Mosque of Ar Rifa'i ❺** (daily 9am–5pm; free, but small charge for royal tombs). Similarly grand in size but less successful, this neo-Mamluk type mosque was built between 1869–1912; the mosque houses various dignitaries and royals, including King Farouk and Iran's last Shah.

BAB AL AZAB

Return to the square and walk past the striped facade of the 16th-century **Mosque of Mahmud Pasha**. Across from the mosque is the **Bab Al Azab** ❻ (Meadan Salah Addin; free), built by the Ottomans as their main gate. It was here in 1811 that Muhammad Ali, in order to assure his position as Pasha of Egypt, massacred 470 Mamluk *beys* (leaders) after inviting them to a banquet. On the leaders' way out, the gates swung shut and Muhammad Ali's soldiers opened fire. Just up the street, opposite the Citadel's northern wall, is the **Al Khadawi** café, see Ⓨ①.

THE CITADEL

Despite keen competition from Cairo's burgeoning skyscrapers, the **Citadel** ❼ (Al Qal'ah; Shari' Salah Salim; tel: 02-2512 1735; daily 8am–5pm, summer until 6pm; free) still dominates the city's skyline. Containing a collection of mosques and palaces (with only reasonably interesting museums), the Citadel is more imposing from the outside, though the views (from the Citadel's terraces) all the way to the pyramids are undeniably impressive.

In order to defend the city against the Crusaders, the great Salah Addin built the citadel in 1176. Spreading over a spur of the Muqattam hills in the east of the city, it is the largest fortification in all the Middle East.

For over 700 years, the Citadel was also the seat of Egypt's rulers who greatly added to and expanded it, notably the Mamluks and Ottomans, until that it is, the arrival of Muhammad Ali (the Ottoman mercenary who schemed his way to power). He demolished almost every one of the old monuments. When Ismail, Ali's grandson, relocated to the Qasr 'bdin (Abdin Palace), the Citadel was relegated to serve as garrison, including to the British during World War II.

The Citadel's Mosques

Much the largest mosque is the vast **Mosque of Muhammad Ali** (Jami' Muhammad 'Ali), which took over 20 years to build. Completed in 1848, it is classic Ottoman in design with its repeating domes and pencil minarets. Faced in alabaster, it's lavish, but singularly lacks character, originality or artistry. Inside, look for the clock in the *sahn* (central courtyard). It was a gift from King Louis-Philippe of France,

Above from far left: inside the city's largest mosque – the lavish Mosque of Muhammad Ali; dome interior at the Citadel.

Citadel Sights Opening hours for the Citadel's museums, mosques and monuments are the same as for the Citadel itself.

Food and Drink Ⓨ

① AL KHADAYWI
Shari' Al Bab Al Gadid, off Meadan Salah Addin; daily 24hrs
Set in the shadow of the citadel with tables under an awning and sheltered by trees, the Al Khadaywi is a simple but tranquil place that's conveniently located. It sells hot and cold drinks including a refreshing mint tea, but no food.

apparently in gratitude for Egypt's gift to him of the obelisk from Luxor's Temple now set in place de la Concorde in Paris.

Nearby lies the early 14th-century **Mosque of An Nassir Muhammad.** The quarter's last remaining Mamluk monument, the mosque is notable for its cedarwood ceiling and the unusual faïence-faced finials of the minarets. Don't miss the **views** from the terrace opposite the entrance to the mosque.

Other Attractions

Also of note here, at the northern end of the terrace, is the **Military Museum (Qasr Al Harim)**, which includes an interesting display of murder weapons. Behind the mosque lies **Yusuf's Well** (Bir Yusuf), dating from Salah Addin's times; the spiral staircase that winds nearly 90m/yds down to the Nile was reputedly dug by Christian prisoners.

In the adjacent Northern Enclosure are the **National Military Museum**,

Muhammad Ali's former Harem Palace, with colourful dioramas illustrating Egypt's major battles, and the **Royal Carriage Museum**, whose exhibits show a wide range of styles.

AL AZHAR PARK

Return to Shari' Salah Salim and walk the 1.5km (1 mile) or so north to **Al Azhar Park ❽** (tel: 02-2510 7378; www.alazharpark.com; Mon–Fri 9am– 10pm, Sat–Sun 9am–11pm; charge) or flag down a cab (LE5–10). Opened in 2005 and stretching over 30 hectares (74 acres), Al Azhar is Cairo's first major park and a cool, safe, tranquil and wholly refreshing escape from the city.

Funded by the Aga Khan Trust for Culture (which focuses on the physical, social, cultural and economic revitalisation of communities in the Muslim world), the idea was to provide a much-needed green space, regenerate a run-down area of the city (the park lies on a former rubbish heap) and create new city reservoirs (which also feed the park's numerous water features).

Paths, affording spectacular panoramic views over the city, criss-cross the formal gardens; there's also a small open-air theatre, a playground and several eating options, including the **Citadel View Restaurant** *(see p.117)* and the cheaper **Trianon**, see ⑪②. Alternatively, bring your own refreshments and take advantage of Cairo's best spot for a picnic.

COPTIC CAIRO

Coptic Cairo is one of the city's hidden jewels. Though small, the quarter boasts several precious churches, an absorbing museum, Egypt's oldest synagogue and its first mosque. Showcasing a very different side of the city, the enclave is also atmospheric, picturesque and peaceful.

Known locally as Misr Al Qadimah (Cairo the Old), Coptic Cairo is one of the oldest continuously inhabited neighbourhoods in the city, with settlements dating back to the 6th century BC. In the 2nd century BC, the Romans chose it as the site of a fortress known as 'Babylon-in-Egypt'.

As the name indicates, the area was once the centre of a large and flourishing Christian community, including a 13th-century icon 'factory' and at least two dozen churches that were much visited by medieval pilgrims. Today, just a cluster remains.

COPTIC MUSEUM

Housed in a Moorish-style palace, Cairo's **Coptic Museum ❶** (Shari' Mari Girgis; tel: 02-2363 7942; www.copticmuseum.gov.eg; daily 9am–5pm; charge) gives a great overview of Coptic history and art with interesting, well-captioned and sometimes beautiful exhibits ranging from Roman times right up to the modern day. Highlights are the monastery frescoes, the tapestry fragments and the illuminated manuscripts.

> **DISTANCE** 1.5km (1 mile)
> **TIME** A half-day
> **START** Coptic Museum
> **END** Mosque of 'Amr Ibn Al'ass
> **POINTS TO NOTE**
> Much the fastest way to reach the Coptic quarter is by metro, taking Line 1 to Mari Girgis station, which lies bang opposite the Coptic Museum. Dress conservatively.

HANGING CHURCH

Approximately 20m/yds south of the museum is the Church of the Blessed Virgin Mary, popularly known as the **Hanging Church ❷** (Al Kanissah Al Mu'allaqah; Shari' Mari Girgis; tel: 02-2363 6305; daily 9am–5pm; free) so named for 'hanging' over a bastion belonging to Roman Babylon, the remains of the old Roman fortress.

Dating to the 7th century, the church is dedicated to the Virgin Mary; a 10th-century icon hangs on the right. A flight of steep steps leads to the ornate 19th-century facade. Inside, the church has a beautiful barrel-vaulted roof, cedarwood

Roman Babylon

As you exit Mari Girgis metro station, look for the remains of two impressive Roman towers and wall fragments built by the emperors Augustus and Trajan, which formed part of the fortress's original gates.

Coptic Mass

If you're interested in learning about the Copts or Coptic liturgy and music (believed to have evolved directly from pharaonic rites and rituals), the Coptic Mass at the Hanging Church provides a memorable introduction (Fri–Sat 8–11/11.30am, Wed 8–9.30am).

panelling and white marble pulpit with 13 elegant columns said to represent Christ and the Apostles. As in the layout of pharaonic temples, the inner sanctum is hidden from public view, but here with delicate 13th-century screens inlaid with ivory. Look out for the glass panel in the baptistery floor, which reveals the Roman bastion.

ST GEORGE'S

Outside the church, take a right on Shari' Mari Girgis, back past the Coptic Museum, and after 70m/yds on the right

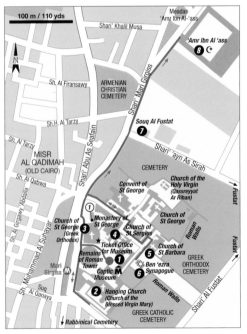

is the circular Greek-Orthodox **Church of St George** ❸ (daily 8am–4pm; free). After the original church was destroyed by fire, it was rebuilt in 1909. The associated monastery, the seat of the Greek patriarch, is not open to the public. At the foot of the church, hidden away, lies the **St George Café**, see ⑪①, a peaceful spot for refreshments.

ST SERGIUS'S

Back on Shari' Mari Girgis, take the steps 10m/yds to the right that lead down to a partly covered alleyway, filled with book stalls. Follow the alleyway (and arrow signs) to the end and, as it veers right, look for a low arch and entrance to the **Church of St Sergius** ❹ (Abu Sarga; daily 8am–4pm; free), dedicated to two martyred Roman soldiers from Syria.

Cairo's oldest church, St Sergius's is thought to date to the 7th century AD, though the current building is an 11th-century restoration, built on the site where the Holy Family are said to have sheltered in a cave during the Flight to Egypt. Stairs near the altar lead down to the crypt, believed to be the site of the cave.

The interior, with its basilica design of three aisles and a central apse, wooden roof and altar screen, is typical of early Coptic churches. Look out for the greatly faded but evocative faces of the Apostles painted on the pillars, thought to date to the 13th century.

ST BARBARA'S

Around 50m/yds along to the left is the **Church of St Barbara** ❺ (daily 8am–4pm; free), dating to the 8th century, but restored in the 12th century. It also follows the classic early church design, and boasts a beautiful marble pulpit and 13th-century altar screen. The saint's relics are kept here.

BEN 'EZRA SYNAGOGUE

To the right of St Barbara's is Egypt's oldest synagogue, the sumptuously restored **Ben 'ezra Synagogue** ❻ (daily 9am–4pm; free), which once served as a 4th-century church. It was here that Moses is said to have been found in a basket, and where the Prophet Jeremiah preached following the destruction of Jerusalem's Great Temple.

SOUQ AL FUSTAT AND THE ARMENIAN CEMETERY

Returning to Shari' Mari Girgis and walking around 100m/yds to the right,

you'll pass **Souq Al Fustat** ❼ (daily 10am–6pm) on the right, where you can buy original, high-quality, traditional handicrafts, some made by charitable organisations. On the other side of the road, look out for the old **Armenian Christian Cemetery**.

MOSQUE OF AMR IBN AL 'ASS

Another 100m/yds on past the bus station is the **Mosque of Amr Ibn Al 'ass** ❽ (Jami' Amr Ibn Al'ass; daily 7am–5pm; free). The site of Egypt's first mosque, built in AD 641, it was named after the Arab general who introduced Islam. Nothing remains of the original, however, and subsequent buildings have been much added to. Women should use the left-hand entrance.

Food and Drink 🍴

① ST GEORGE CAFÉ
Mari Girgis; daily 8am–4pm; £
With shaded seating scattered around the church's outbuildings, this café serves hot and cold drinks (including fresh fruit juices), pizza and sandwiches, including *felafel*, amid the cooing doves.

The Copts

Defined as 'Egyptian Christians', the Copts boast both direct descent from the Ancient Egyptians and one of the earliest adoptions of Christianity. Today, the Copts comprise around 10 percent of Egypt's population. Egyptian Christians separated from the Orthodox Church of the Byzantine Empire in 451, following a dispute over Christ's nature (the Copts believe Christ is monophysite – wholly divine – not both human and divine). Copts contributed invaluably to the development of early Christian doctrine and theology, and are also credited with the creation of monasticism. Today, the Copts are particularly known for forming two major social groups: an educated elite, often wealthy and influential, and some of Egypt's poorest members of society including the *zabbaleen*, Cairo's rubbish collectors.

ALEXANDRIA

Atmospheric and relaxed, Alexandria is a breath of fresh air (literally) after Cairo. This full-day tour includes all the highlights, from famous Roman ruins and catacombs to Arab-era (640–1517) forts and colonial relics, not forgetting a sampling of the city's Old-World cafés and fabled fish.

The Pharos

Keen to promote trade and boost his city's fortunes, Ptolemy II commissioned a great tower that would guide merchant-seamen safely to the city. Completed in 279 BC, it rose to 125m (410ft) high; the Romans later added a giant, oil-burning lamp. With its square base, octagonal central section and circular top, Alexandria's Pharos quickly became an icon and a Wonder of the Ancient World. Withstanding seas, storms and floods for nearly 17 centuries, it was finally floored by a violent earthquake in 1303.

> **DISTANCE** 3 miles (5km)
> **TIME** A full day
> **START** National Museum of Alexandria
> **END** New Library of Alexandria
> **POINTS TO NOTE**
> Trains depart Cairo regularly from 6am and return until around 10pm, taking 2–3 hours. Book tickets at least one day in advance at Rameses station, Cairo (for a small fee, your hotel will send someone). To do this trip in a day, take one of the earliest and faster trains (such as the *Turbini*, *Espani* or *Faransaw*; www.egyptrail.gov.eg). Note there's little difference in comfort between first and second class. On arrival, take a taxi to the National Museum.

The writer Lawrence Durrell dubbed Alexandria 'the Capital of Memory' – an apt moniker for a city with such an illustrious past, but so little to show for it. Alexander the Great's capital, the seat of Cleopatra's throne, home to one of the ancient world's Seven Wonders *(see margin, left)* and its greatest

library, and among the ancient world's wealthiest ports and most illustrious centres of learning, Alexandria today has a legacy that is unfortunately found either underground or underwater.

MUSEUMS

National Museum of Alexandria

One place that does give you an idea of the city's prestigious past is the **National Museum of Alexandria** ❶ (110 Shari' Tariq Al Hurriyyah; daily 9am–4.30pm; charge), housed in a restored Italianate former-pasha's palace.Digestible, with beautiful exhibits that are well laid out and captioned, the museum gives a vivid overview of the city's once-proud past. The museum is divided chronologically: the basement deals with the pharaonic period, the ground floor the Greco-Roman period (look out for the underwater photographs of marine discoveries), and the top floor, Coptic, Muslim and modern Alexandria.

Greco-Roman Museum

Southwest and currently closed (due to reopen in 2012) is the **Greco-Roman**

Museum ❷ (5 Shari' Al Mathaf Ar Romani; tel: 03-486 5829). It houses around 41,000 artefacts – one of the largest collections of Greek and Roman art in the world.

Royal Jewellery Museum

The **Royal Jewellery Museum** ❸ (27 Shari' Ahmed Yehia Pasha; tel: 03-582 8348; daily 9am–4pm; charge) is about 6.5km (4 miles) east of the museum; take a taxi or tram no. 2 (from Meadan Ramla; get off at the Qasr As Safa stop).

Housing a mesmerising collection belonging to Egypt's last royals, the Farouk family, it more than confirms their reputation for extravagance, profligacy and decadence. Objects on display include gardening tools encrusted with diamonds, a platinum crown studded with sapphires and diamonds and a gold chess set inlaid with diamonds and enamel.

ANCIENT RUINS

Return by taxi or tram to Shari' Tariq Al Hurriyyah and head for the old **Pastroudis Patisserie** ❹, where Law-

Alexandria's Great Library

Founded by Ptolemy I at the end of the 3rd century BC, Alexandria's library became the largest in the ancient world. At its height, it contained 700,000 papyrus rolls, probably realising Ptolemy's dream of collecting a copy of every book in the world. The library helped to cement Alexandria's status as a great city of culture. Over the years, a series of fires destroyed the library, as did anti-pagan purges by Christians and Muslims.

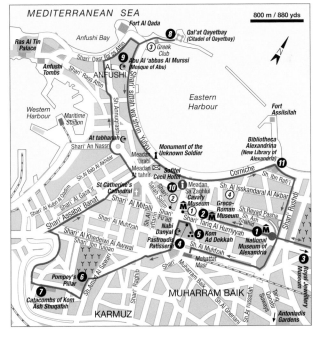

MEDITERRANEAN SEA

800 m / 880 yds

Fort Al Qada

Anfushi Bay

Ras Al Tin Palace

Qal'at Qayetbay (Citadel of Qayetbay) ❽

Greek Club ❸

Shari' Qasr Ras At... Abu Al 'abbas Al Murssi (Mosque of Abu) ❾

Anfushi Tombs

Shari' Rass Attin

AL ANFUSHI

Western Harbour

Maritime Station

Shari' sittah wa 'shrin Yuliu

Sh. Amrurrashu

Eastern Harbour

Fort Assilsilah

At tabharah

Shari' An Nassr

Monument of the Unknown Soldier

Bibliotheca Alexandrina (New Library of Alexandria)

Meadan 'Urabi

Meadan At tahrir

Sofitel Cecil Hotel

Corniche

Sh. Ibn Rafi'i ⓫

Shari' Al Bab Al Akhdar

Shari' Al Kubri Al Qadim

Shari' Al Gaza ir

Shari' Assaba Banat

St Catherine's Cathedral

Shari' Al Mitalli

Shari' Al Muhfzah

Salah Salum

Shari' Al Khedeiwi Al Awwal

Shari' Ibn Tulqan

Meadan Sa'Zaghlui ❿

Cavalry Museum ❷

Shari' Fu'ad

Shari' 'attarin

Nabi Danyal

Pastroudis Patisserie ❹

Meadan Sa'Zaghlui

Greco-Roman Museum

Sh. Al Isskandarat Al Akbar ❹

Sh. Reyad Pasha

Sh. Ash Shahid

Kom Ad Dekkah ❺

Shari' Tariq Al Hurriyyah

Sh. Al Muhfzah

National Museum of Alexandria Ⓜ

Mahattat Masr

Shari' Raghib

Shari' Muharram Baik

Sh. Al Gherian

Sh. Ar russalah

Shari' Al Satwar

Shari' Al Satwar

Pompey's Pillar ❻

Catacombs of Kom Ash Shuqafah ❼

KARMUZ

MUHARRAM BAIK

Tariq, Qanatir Suwayr

Antoniadis Gardens

Royal Jewellery Museum ❸

rence Durrell and the poet of Greek descent C.P. Cavafy used to socialise. For a coffee and a cake in another of Alexandria's famous Old-World cafés, continue along the street for around 250m/yds to **Vinous**, see ⑪①.

Kom Ad Dekkah

Backtrack to Pastroudis, turn left here and then walk across the street to **Kom Ad Dekkah** ❺ (Pile of Rubble); walk around the site to the left and then turn right at the corner for the entrance.

The main monument in this complex is the elegant 2nd-century AD **Roman Amphitheatre** (tel: 03-486 5106; daily 8.30am–4.30pm, closed Fri 11.30am–1.30pm; charge). Though not particularly impressive in size – there are just 13 marble tiers – it is well preserved and is important as the only surviving Roman amphitheatre in Egypt. Look out for the Greek numerals carved into the 'seats'.

At the northern side of the site, in what was once a pleasure garden in Ptolemaic times, is a Roman bath and several Roman villas. A separate entrance ticket allows access to the **Villa of the Birds**, with its nine panels of once-beautiful floor mosaics dating from Hadrian's reign (AD 117–36), though only patches remain today.

Walk back towards Vinous, but at the junction with Shari' Fu'ad, turn left. Less than 100m/yds on the right is **Bistrot**, see ⑪②, a good spot for lunch. After lunch, take a taxi to Pompey's Pillar, the Catacombs of Kom Ash Shuqafah and the Citadel of Qayetbay.

Pompey's Pillar and Serapeum

The mammoth monolith of **Pompey's Pillar** ❻ (Shari' Amud Al Sawari, Karmuz; tel: 03-484 5800; daily 8.30am–4.30pm; charge) is one of the city's best-known landmarks, and towers like a giant tree above the remains of Rhakotis, Alexandria's first settlement. It was dubbed 'Pompey's Pillar' by early visitors; the Roman general was murdered in Alexandria by Cleopatra's brother. However, according to the inscription at the bottom, it was erected in honour of the Roman emperor Diocletian in AD 291 and probably once supported a statue of him.

The 62.8m (206ft) column, two nearby granite sphinxes and a Nilometer (a device for measuring the depth of the Nile; *see p.80*) are all that remain of the once-magnificent **Temple of Serapis**, which, along with the 'overflow' library of Alexandria's Great Library, formed the Serapeum. The library reputedly contained Cleopatra's personal collection of some 200,000 manuscripts. Right up until AD 391, when it was reduced to rubble by the Christians, the Serapeum ranked among the most important religious and intellectual centres in the entire Roman Empire.

CATACOMBS

Turn right out of the Serapeum, take the first street on the right and continue straight up the sloping street for approximately 150m/yds to the Roman **Catacombs of Kom Ash Shuqafah** ❼ (tel: 03-484 5800; daily 8am–4.30pm; charge). These quite extensive 2nd-century AD catacombs were discovered by chance when a donkey pulling a cart suddenly fell through the ground. Cool, completely silent and labyrinthine, they represent the largest Roman burial site in Egypt. They are also typical of the unusual Alexandrian blend of Ancient Egyptian, Greek and Roman styles – look out for the Egyptian gods Anubis and Sobek dressed up as Roman legionaries.

CITADEL OF QAYETBAY

From here it is a swift taxi ride across town to the renovated **Citadel of Qayetbay** ❽ (Qal'at Qayetbay; tel: 03-486 5106; daily 9am–4pm; charge), on the western end of the Corniche. Modern and Disneyesque, the fort in fact dates from the 15th century. Named after its builder, the Mamluk Sultan Qayetbay, it stands on the site of the famous Pharos *(see margin, p.60)*. If you look carefully, you may be able to spot lumps of granite that once formed part of the Pharos and were reused for the citadel.

Cleopatra

Born in Alexandria in 69 BC, Cleopatra showed early signs of her famous shrewdness, ruthlessness and ambition. At the age of 18, she pushed aside her jointly ruling younger brother and took full control of Egypt's affairs. Realising the importance of an alliance with then-dominant Rome, she set about seducing first Julius Caesar (reputedly having herself delivered in a carpet) and, upon his assassination, Mark Antony (making a dramatic entrance dressed as the Greek goddess of love, Aphrodite). She had children with both men. Following her and Mark Antony's defeat at the hands of Octavian (later Emperor Augustus), she killed herself with an asp. Cleopatra and Mark Antony's tombs have never been found, though, excitingly, archaeological excavations currently under way at Taposiris Magna, 50km (31 miles) west of Alexandria, have unearthed new tombs with deep shafts that experts believe might just lead to their discovery. Moreover, coins and a bust of Cleopatra have been unearthed nearby.

From the crenellated walls, there are sweeping views over the Bay of Alexandria, but the interior's not particularly exciting if you are running short of time. The nearby **White & Blue Restaurant**, see ③, is great place for a beer accompanied by some seafood tapas or an early supper.

THE CORNICHE

From the Citadel it is a lovely stroll in the late afternoon back to the centre. Or, hop in a calèche (carriage) to clip-clop down the Corniche (coastal road).

Just beyond the fort is a colourful fishing harbour and boatyard. On the right after about 500m/yds, past some lovely dilapidated colonial houses, is the multi-domed, multi-minareted, light and frothy **Mosque of Abu Al 'abbas**

Above: Citadel exterior, and interior detail; on the Corniche.

Al Murssi ❾ *(daily 7am–dusk; free)*, dedicated to the 13th-century patron saint of Alexandria's sailors and fishermen. Though it was only constructed in 1943, the mosque is built on the site of earlier one, and is impressive for its scale and pleasing proportions.

About 1km (⅔ mile) further along and guarded by soldiers is the **Monument of the Unknown Soldier** on Meadan 'Urabi. Behind it lies **Meadan At Tahrir**, the heart of Alexandria's European city.

Further east is the once-grand **Sofitel Cecil Hotel** ❿ *(see p.112)*, immortalised in Lawrence Durrell's *Alexandria Quartet*, and where Winston Churchill is said to have planned World War II (from the hotel's 'Monty Bar'). Though the renovation has done it no favours, it remains an atmospheric memorial to the Belle Epoque and a good place for a pre-prandial drink or cocktail.

Further along the Corniche is the **New Library of Alexandria** ⓫ (Bibliotheca Alexandrina; www.bibalex. org; Sun–Thur 11am–7pm, Fri–Sat 3–7pm; charge), inaugurated in 2002 and already an icon of 21st-century architecture and a major cultural centre hosting international events.

Lying inland around 400m/yds due south of the Library is **Hud Gondol Seafood**, see ④, the perfect place for a quick fish supper, before walking or catching a cab back to the station. If you decide to overnight in Alexandria, *see Accommodation p.112.*

Food and Drink

③ WHITE & BLUE RESTAURANT

Hellenic Nautical Club, Shari' Qasr Qayetbay, Corniche, Anfushi; tel 03-480 2690; daily noon to midnight; ££
Over 100 years old, the 'Greek Club', as it is popularly known, is something of an institution, famous as much for its stunning views as for its fresh fish and seafood served on its breezy, taverna-style terrace. (Note that food must be consumed with alcohol.)

④ HUD GONDOL SEAFOOD

Corner Shari' Omar Lofti Muhammad Motwe, Shatbi; tel 03-476 1779; daily noon to midnight; £
This restaurant is hidden down a side street, and you may have to ask doggedly for directions to find it. It's definitely worth the effort, however. Much loved locally, Hud Gondol is basic and noisy, with no menus and little English spoken, but is *the* place to come for fresh seafood at unbeatable prices.

LUXOR – EAST BANK

The monumental temple complexes of Karnak and Luxor (Al Uqsur, in Arabic) rank among the world's greatest ancient sites. In terms of artistic achievement, they are Egypt's finest; in scale, its most impressive. Beautiful artefacts found on site are displayed in two worthwhile museums.

Ancient Thebes, Luxor's ancient ancestor, was one of the greatest cities of the ancient world. Serving as the political capital of ancient Egypt during the Middle and New Kingdoms (2160–1064 BC), the city benefited from the splendid patronage of some of Egypt's most powerful pharaohs, among them Sety I, Rameses II and Queen Hatshepsut.

Then, as now, the city staddles both banks of the Nile. The East Bank, where the sun rises, is the site of temples and palaces; the land of the living. The West, where the sun sinks, has tombs and necropolises; the land of the dead.

KARNAK TEMPLE

From the centre of town, follow the Corniche An Nil northwards to **Karnak Temple of Amun-Ra ❶** (Shari' Al Karnak; daily 6am–5.30pm, summer to 6pm; charge). On the way, just past Luxor Hospital on the right, is the compound of **Chicago House**. Home to the Oriental Institute of Chicago University, it has been recording monuments and finds in and around Luxor since 1924.

DISTANCE 7.5km (5 miles)
TIME A full day
START Karnak Temple
END Luxor Museum
POINTS TO NOTE
Head for Karnak as early in the day as possible in order to visit the temple during the relative cool and tour-group-free peace of the morning. This tour can be walked – Karnak lies only around 2.5km (1½ miles) north of Luxor centre – or take a calèche (from LE20–40 per hour; be sure to negotiate the price before jumping in) or a taxi (LE5–10, depending on the length of the journey). *For information on getting to Luxor, see p.107.*

Known as Ipet-Isut (Most Perfect of Places) to the Ancient Egyptians, Karnak was dedicated to the city's most powerful triad: the god Amun, his consort Mut (the Mistress of Heaven) and their son Khonsu, the moon-god.

Covering some 40 hectares (100 acres), Karnak is a vast site. For more

Above from far left:
Alexandria's Corniche;
Karnak Temple.

Above: Karnak Temple, details of which are shown above, spreads across some 40 hectares (100 acres).

Opet Festival

Once a year during the grand Opet festival, the statue of Amun was ceremoniously transported by boat from Karnak to Luxor Temple. Here, Amun was reunited with his consort, Mut, amid much celebration. The re-enaction of this annual ritual was considered essential by pharaohs, priesthood and people in order to ensure the fertility of the land for the coming year.

than 1,500 years it was the most important religious and intellectual centre in Ancient Egypt. Every pharaoh wished to leave his mark on the sacred site, building, embellishing, enlarging or simply restoring the temples of the complex. Such additions and embellishments can make the layout, style and chronology of the temple seem confusing, but, as a basic rule of thumb, the further you penetrate into the monument, the older the remnants.

The **Precinct of Amun** is the easiest area to comprehend, and the best place to start. From the ticket office, head along the **Processional Way**. The avenue of ram-headed sphinxes (one of the representations of Amun) leads to the huge but unfinished **First Pylon**.

To the left of the large Forecourt is **Sety II's shrine** (1199–1193 BC), which held the triad deities' sacred boats, and to the right the beautiful **Temple of Rameses III** (1182–1151 BC), a classic pharaonic temple in style, decorated with scenes of the Opet festival *(see margin, left)*.

The **Second Pylon** is guarded by the colossus of Rameses II, with one of his daughters at his feet. Next, the **Great Hypostyle Hall**, begun by Amenhotep III (1386–1349 BC),

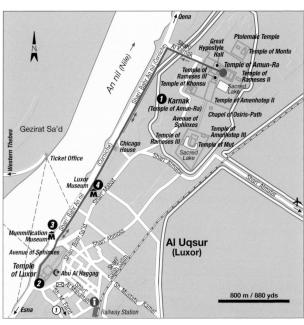

continued by Sety I (1296–1279 BC) and finished by his son Rameses II (1279–1212 BC), is considered one of the architectural marvels of Ancient Egypt. The hypostyle hall in a temple traditionally represents a garden; in this case, it's more like a forest, with 134 enormous columns spreading over 5,500 sq m (59,000 sq ft).

On the northern side, dating from the time of Sety I, are exquisite **bas-reliefs**; those on the south walls date from the reign of Rameses II (the pharaoh known for 'quantity over quality') and, typically, are much more crudely finished.

Further along this axis are the **obelisks of Thutmose III** (*c*.1479–*c*.1425 BC) and the **Obelisk of Queen Hatshepsut** (*c*.1472–*c*.1457 BC), his stepmother and one of the only female pharaohs to rule Egypt *(see p.24–5)*.

Housed in the granite **Sanctuary of Amun** was the sacred statue of the god. Scenes in the sanctuary show the priests making offerings in Amun's honour.

Near the obelisks you cross the temple's secondary axis, which runs past the **Sacred Lake**, four more pylons and the **Cachette Court**, where thousands of statues were excavated in 1903.

After visiting Karnak, take a calèche or walk the 10 minutes to **Sofra**, see ⑪①, where you can have an alfresco Egyptian lunch. For something simpler or faster, try **Oasis Cafe**, see ⑪②, lying around 650m/yds north of the Temple of Luxor.

TEMPLE OF LUXOR

After lunch, return to the Corniche, and on to the **Temple of Luxor** ❷ (daily 6am–9pm, summer to 10pm; charge). Like Karnak, the temple was dedicated to the mighty Theban triad of Amun, Mut and Khonsu.

The core of the temple was built by Amenhotep III (1390–1352 BC), and even though it was embellished and expanded several times, its plan remains much simpler and more compact than the complex in Karnak.

Mosque of Yusuf Al Haggag

Until 1885, the temple was entirely buried under the modern town of Luxor. Only the monumental heads of the Rameses colossi and the tips of the obelisks rose out of the rubble. When excavations started, Luxor's vil-

Above from far left: hieroglyphics and ruins at Karnak Temple, dedicated to the god Amun, his consort Mut (the Mistress of Heaven) and their son Khonsu, the moon-god.

Animal Mummies Mummification, which took up to 70 days, was not restricted to humans. Various animals underwent the process too; most commonly these included bulls, rams, crocodiles and cats.

Food and Drink 🍴

① SOFRA

90 Shari' Muhammad Farid, behind the Old Winter Palace, East Bank; tel: 095-235 9752; www.sofra.co.eg; £–££
With its diminutive dining rooms and funky decor, mostly sourced from local junk markets, Sofra's a quirky, intimate and friendly little place, serving fresh Egyptian food at excellent prices. There's also a lovely roof terrace. No alcohol is served, but there's a good selection of fresh fruit juice.

② OASIS CAFE

Shari' Dr Labib Habashi, East Bank; tel: 095-336 7121; £–££
Occupying a renovated 1930s house in the centre of town, this café-cum-restaurant serves decent coffee and a good range of international dishes in peaceful and laid-back surroundings, often to the tunes of jazz or Sufi music.

Above: Luxor Temple decoration; Sound and Light Show *(see below)*.

Sound and Light Show
Karnak hosts its own, two-part Sound and Light Show (tel: 02-3385 2880; www.soundandlight.com.eg; charge), which begins with a walk through the floodlit temple, then winds up at the theatre beyond the Sacred Lake. Cheesy it may be, but it's a great chance to see the temple at night. The Temple of Luxor (until 10pm) is also floodlit nightly.

lagers were relocated and their homes pulled down. One building remained: the **Mosque of Yusuf Abu Al Haggag**, dedicated to Luxor's patron saint. Today it remains where it has always been: perched on the roof of the hypostyle hall. Every year on the saint's day *(moulid)*, the people of Luxor drag several boats up to the mosque, a ritual not unlike the one performed for millennia during the Opet festival *(see margin, p.66)*.

Avenue of Sphinxes
As 'the Harem of the South', as it was known, Luxor was connected to Karnak by a 3km (2-mile) long processional **Avenue of Sphinxes**, part of which is still visible, the rest of which is currently undergoing excavation. Eventually, it will be renovated in its entirety all the way to Karnak.

Monuments of Rameses II
In front of the **First Pylon**, built by Rameses II, stands an **obelisk** and four **colossi**. Originally there were two obelisks, but one was shipped to France and now graces place de la Concorde in Paris.

Rameses II decorated the First Pylon with a much-loved subject, his purported victory in the Battle of Qadesh (in fact, the world's first peace treaty was signed following a stalemate).

The large **Court of Rameses II** is surrounded by two rows of papyrus-bud columns and further colossi of the self-deifying pharaoh.

The **barque shrine** (where a sacred boat was kept when not in use) to the right, in fact built during an earlier period by Thutmose III, has three chapels dedicated to the Theban triad. On the walls to the right are some fine reliefs of a funerary procession led by Rameses II's many sons (he was said to have fathered nearly 200 sons and daughters), and of the temple itself.

Monuments of Amenhotep
Beyond the Second Pylon is the **Processional Colonnade of Amenhotep III** with its beautiful papyrus columns, on which the Great Hypostyle Hall at Karnak was modelled. The walls were decorated during the reign of Tutankhamun with scenes of the Opet celebrations.

Perhaps even more impressive is the **Great Sun Court of Amenhotep III**, damaged in recent decades due to rising water-tables. During restoration works in 1989, archaeologists discovered a large cache of statues, which are now on show at the Luxor Museum *(see opposite)*. Much later, the columned portico was used by Roman soldiers as a chapel.

Behind it lies the **Inner Sanctuary of Amun's Barge**, built by Alexander the Great; to the left is **Amenhotep III's Birth Room**, with scenes that show the pharaoh's divine conception, as well as his suckling by several goddesses.

Ancient Egyptians believed that the rock on which this part of the temple stands was the exact spot where the god Amun was born.

LUXOR'S MUSEUMS

Mummification Museum

From the Temple of Luxor, cross the Corniche to visit the small **Mummification Museum** ❸ (tel: 095-238 1501; daily, winter 9am–1pm and 4–9pm, summer 9am–1pm and 5–10pm; charge). It may not sound terribly enthralling, but this little museum is actually most imaginatively designed and gives an interesting overview of the elaborate mummification process. Exhibits are carefully chosen and include a mummified ram, some mummies and the simultaneously delicate and gruesome-looking mummification instruments themselves.

Luxor Museum

Continue along the Corniche, either walking or by taxi, to the outstanding **Luxor Museum** ❹ (tel: 095-238 0269; daily, winter 9am–9pm, summer 9am–1pm and 5–10pm). Among the small but select collection of ancient artefacts, the many highlights include the splendid statues of the young King Thutmose III and Amenhotep III held by Sobek, the crocodile-god. Equally impressive are the fine heads of the rebel pharaoh Akhenaten and other objects emanating from his temple in Karnak following its destruction by later pharaohs trying to eradicate his memory. The **New Hall** has a display of the cache of statues found in the Temple of Luxor.

At the back of the temple is the entrance to the colourful **souq**, ideal for a relaxed, late-afternoon stroll or shopping spree.

A great spot to rest sightseeing-weary legs is the **Coffee Shop Oum Koulsoum**, see ⑪③, or for a cooling cocktail in civilised surroundings, head straight for the **Nile Terrace Bar**, see ⑪④. For dinner, try the nearby **Kebabgy**, see ⑪⑤.

Above from far left: bird's-eye view of Luxor Temple by night; obelisk detail at Luxor Temple.

Food and Drink 🍴

③ COFFEE SHOP OUM KOULSOUM
Shari' As Souk; tel: 095-378 2194; daily 24hrs; £
Located on a pleasant terrace in the thick of the souq, the Oum Koulsoum's a great place to people-watch over an *asab* (sugar-cane juice) or a *sheesha*.

④ NILE TERRACE BAR
Sofitel Old Winter Palace, Corniche An Nil; tel: 095-238 0421; daily noon–midnight; £££
The best place in Luxor for a sun-downer, or to watch the feluccas perform their daily sunset dance, are the two raised terraces of the Sofitel Old Winter Palace hotel *(see p.114)*. Cocktails, spirits and beer are all served, as are snacks.

⑤ KEBABGY
New Lower Corniche, opposite the Sofitel Old Winter Palace, East Bank; tel: 095-238 652; ££–£££
The Kebabgy offers Egyptian, Middle Eastern and international dishes, with specials ranging from stuffed pigeon to duck *à l'orange*.

LUXOR – WEST BANK

Littered with tombs and temples, shrines and statues, Luxor's West Bank boasts what could be described as an embarrassment of riches. Monuments to the dead they may be, but the monuments here bring to life the daily activities, pleasures and concerns of the Ancient Egyptians like nowhere else.

DISTANCE 12km (7½ miles)
TIME A full day
START Colossi of Memnon
END Temple of Rameses II
POINTS TO NOTE

Start the tour as early as possible. If you go by taxi, hire one for the day. If you go by bike, these can be rented in town or at one of the hotels. Check the bike's condition and whether it's comfortable, as the journey can be arduous. Bikes can be taken with you on the public ferry (small charge) opposite the Temple of Luxor. Tickets for some sites are sold only at the ticket office at the crossroads to the left, past the Colossi of Memnon. Otherwise, tickets are available at each site's entrance, but check at the ticket office first. Tickets for the Valley of the Kings are for three tombs only; if you want to visit more, you should buy two tickets. Most West Bank sites open daily in summer 6am–5pm, winter 9am–4.30pm, and charge fees. Bring a torch and comfortable shoes.

Up, Up and Away

Well run, with a good safety record, Hod-Hod Soliman (Shari' Omar Ali, near Shari' At Televiziuun, Luxor; tel: 095-227 1116; hodhodoffice@yahoo. co.uk) organises balloon trips over the West Bank. The views of the monuments are terrific. Prices are £95/76 in winter/ summer for around a 50-minute ride. The company can transfer you (for free) to and from your hotel.

The place of the setting sun, Luxor's West Bank was devoted to the dead. Pharaohs and kings opted to be buried in the secluded and secret Valley of the Kings; their nobles, princes, ministers and viziers chose the Valley of the Nobles, opposite their masters. In between lie spectacular and conspicuous mortuary temples built by the pharaohs, including the Madinat Habu, Dair Al Bahari and the Ramesseum.

For a memorable overview – literally – of the monuments, you can't beat an early-morning **hot-air balloon ride** over the West Bank *(see margin, left)*. Return to the hotel for breakfast. After that, take the public ferry back to the West Bank, then cycle or take a taxi from the

Food and Drink

① DREAMS OF MEMNON
Opposite the Colossi of Memnon; tel: 095-206 0657; daily 24hrs; £
Though newly opened and still requiring some TLC, Dreams is a very welcoming spot serving simple but fresh meals at rock-bottom prices. Dishes include fish and chicken *tagen* and couscous, and a variety of salads.

ferry terminal towards the mountains to the Colossi of Memnon. If you prefer to stay on the West Bank after a balloon ride, then **Dreams of Memnon**, see ⑪①, is a good place to head for a late breakfast or a soft drink.

COLOSSI OF MEMNON

Sitting serenly amid sugar-cane fields, the huge statues that are the **Colossi of Memnon** ❶ (Shari' Memnon; 24hrs; free) are all that remain of Amenhotep III's temple, once among the largest and most magnificent of the West Bank. The misnomer comes from the Ancient Greeks, who believed that these statues represented the legendary king Memnon.

VALLEY OF THE KINGS

At the next crossroads, buy your tickets from the office on the corner, then head for the **Valley of the Kings** ❷ (Biban Al Muluk; charge for a choice of up to three tombs excluding those of Ay and Tutankhamun – extra charge applies), following the road parallel to the mountains (the site is signposted).

Above from far left: a novel way to see the Nile (see margin, opposite); the Colossi of Memnon.

Desert Tombs

From c.2150 BC, the pharaohs chose to be buried in tombs and not pyramids. Their choice of site was the barren and secluded Valley of the Kings, northwest of Thebes (Luxor's ancient ancestor). Royal burials continued here for the next 500 years. The elaborate tombs, designed to resemble the underworld, were cut into the rock, then decorated with vivid scenes and texts to assist the dead kings in the afterlife. A pharaoh would start working on his tomb as soon as he became king, but often died before its completion.

Map labels

Valley of the Kings
1 Rameses VI
2 Thutmose III
3 Rameses III
4 Tutankhamun
5 Sety I
6 Montu-Hir-Khopsef

Amenhotep III
Ay
Valley of the Kings (Biban Al Muluk) ❷
Tomb of the Royal Cache
Tomb & Temple of Mentuhotep Sa'ankhkara
Tombs of the Nobles (Shaykh Abd Al Qurnah) ❺
Valley of the Queens (Wadi Al Malekat)
Dair Al Madinah (Workers' Village)
Qurnet Mura'i
1 Nefertari
2 Amenherchopeshef
3 Teti
4 Khaemwaset
Madinat Habu ❹
Temple of Ay & Horemheb
Temple of Rameses III
Temple of Amun
Palace of Amenhotep III
Temple of Thutmose III
Birkat Habu (Site of Lake of Amenhotep III)
Al Kom

Dair Al Bahari
Temple of Hatshepsut ❸
Temple of Mentuhotep
Causeway of Hatshepsut
Tombs of Late Period
Al Asasif
Shaykh Abd Al Qurnah ❸
Ptolemaic Temple
Temple of Tawseret
Temple of Merenptah
Temple of Amenhotep, Son of Hapu
Temple of Thutmose II
Colossi of Memnon ❶①

Howard Carter's House
Tombs of the Nobles
Drah Abu Annaja
Temple of Rameses IV
Temple of Thutmose III
Temple of Amenophis II
Temple of Rameses II (Ramesseum) ❹
Temple of Thutmose IV
Necropolis of Thebes (Western Thebes)
Al Qurnah Al Jadidah (New Village)

Temple of Sety I
Al-Qurna

Al Faddiyah Canal
Luxor–East Bank

Ticket Office ❷
Esna, Al Nakhil

800 m / 880 yds
N

Tomb Robbers

The entrances to most tombs were carefully concealed, their location and construction a fiercely guarded secret. Even in ancient times, however, robbers posed a problem, and guards were often posted to deter them. The punishment if caught was severe: impalement on a stake. Despite the precautions, almost all the pharaonic tombs were plundered.

On the crossroads near the cemetery, the mud-brick house on the hill to the right was Howard Carter's home while he excavated Tutankhamun's tomb *(see feature, below)*.

There are 63 tombs in the Valley of the Kings, but not all are open; tombs rotate opening times in order to reduce the exposure of the wall decorations to humidity caused by human breath and perspiration. Most people visit no more than five. One of the most popular, the **Tomb of Tutankhamun** (separate entry ticket available at the tomb) is one of the smallest and least decorated.

The latest and largest tomb to be discovered, **KV5**, is still being excavated by the American archaeologist Kent Weeks. So far, he and his team have found more than 110 rooms, which would have housed more than 50 of Rameses II's sons. The tomb is closed, but you can follow Weeks's progress on his website (www.theban mappingproject.com).

The most splendid tomb, with fine wall carvings, belongs to **Sety I**, but this is closed definitively to the public because of its fragile state. Other tombs worth visiting are the **Tomb of Rameses VI**, the **Tomb of Rameses III** with its painting of musicians, the newly opened **Tomb of Montu-Hir-Khopsef** and, one of the largest, the **Tomb of Thutmose III**.

If you need a pitstop, the shaded rest house near the entrance serves rather overpriced cold drinks and snacks.

Tutankhamun's Treasures

On 4 November 1922, a boy water-carrier working for a British archaeologist named Howard Carter stumbled upon a stone step in the desert. It led to a sunken staircase. Having excavated in the valley with little success for several years, and with his patron, Lord Carnarvon, rapidly running out of both patience and funds, Carter experienced enormous relief at the discovery of the boy-pharaoh's tomb. On 25 November, in the presence of Carter's patron, the tomb's door was finally opened. Filled from floor to ceiling with gleaming treasures, the tomb contained not just priceless jewellery and a solid gold funerary mask, but huge quantities of ordinary objects, ranging from plates of food and favourite toys, to weapons and games. Given that this was the treasure interred with a minor pharaoh, you can only wonder at the treasure once buried with pharaohs as powerful as Sety I or his son Rameses II.

DAIR AL BAHARI AND THE TEMPLE OF HATSHEPSUT

Return to the main road, then take the first road to the right. Turn right again for **Dair Al Bahari**, the site of the **Mortuary Temple of Queen Hatshepsut** ❸ (charge).

Set dramatically against the Theban hills, the temple appears startlingly modern. In Queen Hatshepsut's day (1472–1457 BC), it would have formed part of a beautiful garden, the Djeser Djeseru ('Sacred of Sacreds'), dedicated to her 'father', the god Amun. The architect, Senenmut, thought to have been the queen's lover, filled the garden with exotic plants and flowers collected during the queen's expeditions to East Africa.

Hatshepsut's stepson, Thuthmose III *(see p.24–5)* hated the queen so much that when he became king he defaced as many of her images, cartouches and monuments as he could, including on this temple. Over time, the wide avenue of sphinxes that once connected the temple to the Nile disappeared, as did much of the Lower Terrace and pylons. The galleries on the **Second Terrace** are decorated with fine reliefs of the queen's divine parentage (in the **Birth Colonnade**). In the Punt Colonnade, look out for the expedition to Punt (today's East Africa), from where myrrh trees, ebony, ivory and spices were brought back. Further south is the **Chapel of Hathor**, with Hathor-headed columns. The

Third Terrace has a portico of Osiride columns (depicting the god Osiris, but with suggestions of the queen), some of which have been restored.

Return to the main road, and turn right. Opposite the ticket office, around 600m/yds south of the Ramesseum, is **Nur Al Gurna**, see ⑪②.

THE RAMESSEUM

After lunch, head for the **Ramesseum** ❹. Rameses II (1279–1212 BC) originally planned his mortuary temple to be grander than anything he had built previously. Unfortunately, the land he chose for it later came to be inundated annually, and his temple fell apart. His colossus, weighing over 900 tons, fell over and smashed the Second Pylon and the Second Court; it now lies in pieces, scattered all over the temple.

The pylons and walls of the **Main Hypostyle Hall** are decorated with scenes of Rameses II's victories, while one of the smaller hypostyle halls has a remarkable ceiling depicting the oldest-known 12-month calendar.

Shelley's Sonnet
The British poet Percy Bysshe Shelley (1792–1822) eternalised the broken colossus of Rameses II in the Ramesseum in his poem *Ozymandias* (another name for Rameses), beginning with the immortal lines: 'I met a traveller from an antique land/Who said: two vast and trunkless legs of stone/Stand in the desert...'

Food and Drink

② NUR AL GURNA
Near ticket office, West Bank; tel: 095-231 1430; daily 8am–8pm; £
With its lovely shaded garden terrace, the peaceful little Gurna is a great place for escaping the sun. Though simple, it's friendly and welcoming and does good Egyptian dishes, including stuffed pigeon, at decent prices. No alcohol.

Book of the Dead

Dating from the New Kingdom, the Book of the Dead was designed to safeguard the deceased in the afterlife, and contained a series of protective spells and incantations. Taking the form of rolled-up papyri bound with strips of linen and sealed with clay, the Book was usually placed in the coffin of the deceased, or depicted in special hieroglyphics and images on the walls of the tombs. A common theme was the 'weighing of the heart' by Anubis to determine whether the deceased was worthy enough to enter the underworld kingdom of Osiris.

The well-preserved vaulted mud-brick structures at the back of the temple were used as workshops, servants' quarters and storage houses. Opposite lies the '**Ramasseum' Café**, see ⑪③.

TOMBS OF THE NOBLES

Cross the road to the **Tombs of the Nobles ❺**. Though the quality of the decorations in these tombs may be inferior to those in the Valley of the Kings, they are far less visited, and in many cases the paintings are in better condition. While the pharaohs decorated their tombs with scenes from the Book of Dead (see margin, left), the nobles chose day-to-day scenes, so shedding light on their ordinary, daily lives.

The tombs furthest west are the **Tomb of Rekhmire**, with scenes of deceased nobles receiving tributes from foreign lands, and the **Tomb of Sennofer** (the 'Tomb of the Vines') with its antechamber painted with vines. The

two styles of carving in the **Tomb of Ramose** show that he was vizier during and after the Amarnah revolution (see p.32–3). Further north, the **Tomb of Nakht** has scenes of Nakht at a banquet with dancers and a blind harpist.

MADINAT HABU

Return to the main road, and continue past the ticket office to the **Temple of Rameses III ❻** at **Madinat Habu**. Rameses III (1182–1151 BC) modelled this temple on his father's Ramesseum – the last grand pharaonic temple built in Egypt.

The upper floor is decorated with dancers and musicians and was probably where the king was entertained by his harem. The massive First and Second Pylons are in fact decorated with the battles fought by Rameses II, not III. The First Court contains fine wall carvings bearing some original colours, but the hypostyle hall and sanctuaries have suffered badly from earthquake damage. Until excavations started in the 19th century, the temple was covered by the remains of the Coptic town of Djeme, of which some mud-brick structures are still visible. Walk around the temple to see the outer wall carvings and the remains of the sacred lake to the north. You can sit at the **Maratonga Cafeteria**, see ⑪④, for a fruit cocktail at sunset. Afterwards, return along the main road to the ferry and cross the Nile.

Food and Drink

③ 'RAMASSEUM' CAFÉ

Opposite the Ramesseum; daily 7am–midnight; £
Currently the only place for cold drinks near the Ramesseum. It serves food, including omelettes, chicken dishes and salad, and regularly stocks Egyptian Stella beer.

④ MARATONGA CAFETERIA

Opposite Madinat Habu; daily 5.30am–6pm; £
With its view of Madinat Habu and cool, shaded tables, this is a pleasant and peaceful place for a fresh fruit juice. Also serves coffee and food.

ABYDOS AND DANDARAH

Lying downstream from their famous 'cousins' at Karnak and Luxor, the temples of Abydos and Dandarah are often overlooked by visitors. But numbering among the most impressive sights on the Nile, with a prestigious past and some exceptional artistry, they are definitely worth remembering.

Dedicated to Osiris, the all-important god of the underworld *(see p.27)*, Abydos was once one of the holiest sites in Egypt. With its exquisite (and well-preserved) reliefs, the Temple of Sety I remains one of Egypt's most finely decorated monuments.

Though dating from a much later period, the Ptolemaic temple of Dandarah is impressive for its excellent state of preservation and atmosphere. An important religious and administrative site, Dandarah was begun by the Ptolemies but completed later, by the Romans.

ABYDOS

From Luxor, the road north to Abydos follows the course of the Nile for 64km (40 miles) to Qena. In spring and early summer, bougainvillaea, magnolia and mimosa line the road. Look out also for farmers cultivating the fields of wheat and sugar cane with their *gamusas* (water buffalos) as they have for millennia.

From Qena, it's another 93km (60 miles) to the small town of **Al Balyana**, where a small road leads 9km (6 miles)

DISTANCE 350km (217 miles)
TIME A full day
START Abydos
END Naqarah
POINTS TO NOTE
At the time of writing, restrictions on independent travel north of Luxor (Al Uqsur) had been lifted, but check with the Tourist Office first. If reimposed, you can take an organised bus tour to Abydos and/or Dandarah from Luxor, or join the regular one-day Nile cruises to Dandarah (both arranged through the town's travel agencies and hotels). Travelling independently, you can take a bus about 30 minutes) or train (around 40 minutes) from Luxor to Qena, then a local bus service or private taxi for the 4km (2½ miles) to Dandarah. Trains and buses run to Al Balyana, from where it's a 10km (6-mile) local bus or taxi ride to Abydos. Faster and simpler (particularly for visiting both temples the same day) is hiring a private taxi for the day at Luxor (from LE400).

Above from far left:
Temple of Rameses III at Madinat Habu; wall art at the Temple of Abydos.

Pilgrimage to Abydos

Like the rest of the Islamic world, Egyptian Muslims aspire to make the pilgrimage to Mecca at least once in their lives. Their forefathers, however, headed for Abydos. Epicentre of the cult of Osiris, it was believed that the god's head was buried here, and that the temple marked the gate of the underworld itself. If the deceased failed to get here during their lifetime, their mummy was sometimes brought here before burial. Sometimes tombs were decorated with imaginary journeys to Abydos.

to the village of **Al Araba Al Madfuna** and **Abydos ❶** (daily 7am–4pm, summer to 5pm; charge).

Temple of Sety I

Grand in scale and concept, the **Temple of Sety** was built by Sety I (1296–1279 BC) both as a testament to his devotion to Osiris, and in order to link himself directly with the kings of the past. The pylon and walls of the first two courts have crumbled. Passing through the first hypostyle hall (completed by Sety's son Rameses II – the decoration is noticeably cruder), you reach the second hypostyle hall, where the famous reliefs are found, including of the king dressed as a priest of the temple.

Unusually, the temple is dedicated to seven deities, each with its own sanctuary. From right to left, they are as follows: Horus, Isis, Osiris, Amun, Ra-Horakhty, Ptah and the deified Sety himself. Fine reliefs also line the sanctuary walls.

Right: sunlight streams into the Temple of Sety I at Abydos.

Leading left off the hall, the first corridor – known as the **Gallery of the Kings** – lists the 76 names of the pharaohs up to Sety I, with a few glaring political exceptions, including the female pharaoh Hatshepsut *(see p.24–5)* and 'the heretic' Akhenaten *(see p.24–5).* Such 'king lists' have proven extremely useful to Egyptologists trying to work out the pharaohs' tricky chronology.

Osireion

Behind the temple and currently under restoration is the **Osireion**, or cenotaph, where Sety's I's mummy rested before burial in the Valley of the Kings. It is currently closed, but when it reopens, look out for the lovely ceiling carving of the goddess Nut.

Temple of Rameses II

Lying some 250m/yds to the east is the limestone **Temple of Rameses II.** Currently closed, it contains well-preserved coloured reliefs, and carved granite and alabaster ornamentation.

After exiting, the **Osiris Park Café**, see ⑪①, makes a convenient spot for refreshments before starting for Dandarah. Shops opposite sell souvenir booklets on Abydos.

DANDARAH

Return to Qena and cross the river for the 4km (2½ miles) to **Dandarah ❷** (daily winter 7am–5pm, summer to 6pm; charge).

Temple of Hathor

Standing on the site of much earlier shrines to Hathor, Dandarah's Greco-Roman temple was built between 125 BC–AD 60 in the classic Ptolemaic style *(see margin, p.89)*.

In the two **hypostyle halls**, look out for the columns bearing Hathor's cow-face as capitals, as well as the colourful ceiling (currently in the process of being cleaned) decorated with stars, gods and signs of the Egyptian zodiac. On the walls of the outer hypostyle hall are scenes of Roman emperors making offerings to the Egyptian gods – to placate priesthood, people and deities. In the **Inner Sanctuary**, which housed the statue of Hathor that was kept in darkness, and had chapels behind, are scenes depicting the pharaoh's ritual offerings to Hathor.

Reliefs on the **stairway** leading to the roof of the temple show the New Year's rituals and celebrations, when Hathor's statue was carried onto the open-air kiosk in the southwestern corner of the roof to be rejuvenated by the sun-god, before reunion with her consort, Horus.

Outside, on the rear (southern) wall of the temple, seek out the **giant reliefs** of Caesarion (son of Cleopatra and Julius Caesar), with the queen herself standing behind her young son.

RETURN TO LUXOR

Return to Luxor via the West Bank and stop 23km (14 miles) south of Qena, at **Al Ballas ③**, a village of potters since antiquity. Further south is **Naqadah ④**, home of Qasr Al Hamam, a mud-brick palace for pigeons reputedly built by a 19th-century monk. A lovely place to stop for a drink, dinner or both is the Al Moudira *(see p.119)*, located just 7km (4 miles) from the bridge.

Above from far left: Temple of Abydos; exterior and interior of the temple at Dandarah.

Above: the ruins at the Greco-Roman temple at Dandarah.

Food and Drink

① OSIRIS PARK CAFÉ

Abydos; daily 6.30am–6pm
Sandwiched strategically between the car park and Temple, the Osiris Park Café provides welcome shade and leg-rest at simple wooden tables under a palm-frond roof. No food is sold, but you can unwrap your picnic and enjoy an ice-cold soft drink or water here.

20 km / 12½ miles

ASWAN TOWN
AND ISLANDS

Palpably hotter than towns further north, and home to the Nubian people, Egypt's Aswan feels like Africa at last. This tour explores Nubian history and culture, a ruined Christian monastery and the remains of a pharaonic city, with a garden and a souq offering diversion along the way.

DISTANCE 15km (9 miles), not including boat trips
TIME A full day
START Monastery of St Simeon
END Aswan Souq
POINTS TO NOTE

Start early. The Monastery of St Simeon is best done first. Though it's a 30- to 40-minute trek by foot or by camel (pre-arranged through your hotel), the desert heat can be ferocious, particularly in summer. A hat, sunscreen and lots of water are essential. Public ferries to/from the Tomb of the Nobles on the West Bank leave about every 15 minutes from an unmarked pier diagonally opposite Aswan's railway station (just before the Alexander the Great Pier). Ferries to Elephantine leave from diagonally opposite the Egypt Air office, docking near Aswan Museum. A ferry also connects the Island's western side with a pier opposite Aswan's telephone exchange.

Getting there
For information on getting to Aswan, see p.107.

see p.107.

In pharaonic times, Aswan played a vital strategic, military and commercial role. Marking Egypt's southern boundary, it served as a fortress town, as well as a launching pad for major military expeditions. Situated at the crossroads of ancient African trading routes, the town has also seen valuable cargo come and go by caravan.

The town has also served as a quarry, furnishing Ancient Egypt with fine granite for the fashioning of some of its greatest sculptures and obelisks.

WEST BANK

For a slice of modern Aswani life, catch a ferry to the West Bank: Nubian women carry herbs to market; school children hurriedly finish homework; old men exchange all the gossip and besuited bureaucrats chat on mobile phones. Note that women are expected to sit at the front of the boat.

Monastery of St Simeon

You don't need a guide to find the monastery; it's visible once you climb

up the hill from the ferry pier. If you're going by camel (from LE30 per hour plus tip for the cameleer), arrange to meet your guide at the pier.

A sacred Christian site since the 7th century, today's **Monastery of St Simeon** ❶ (Dair Al Saman; daily, winter 8am–4pm, summer 7am–5pm; charge) dates to the 10th century. For some 200 years it served as the centre of Christian efforts to convert the pagan populace, until its destruction at the hands of the great Muslim conqueror Salah Addin in the 12th century.

Though just ruins remain, the monastery is impressive for its size (over 300 monks once resided here); its fortress-like appearance, with its 10m/ yd high stone walls to protect against Muslim incursion, and its dramatic desert setting. The guardian will point out traces of original frescoes, and the spot on the ceiling where St Simeon allegedly tied his beard to prevent him from nodding off during prayer.

Aga Khan Mausoleum and Villa
After visiting the monastery (or before if you're running early), you can trek

Above from far left: *The Sudan* Nile cruiser, and Aswan ferries (seen in the background), which connect the mainland with Elephantine Island; the single-domed Aga Khan Mausoleum.

Above: Tomb of the Nobles (see p.80); Aswan Botanical Gardens (see p.83), on Kitchener's Island.

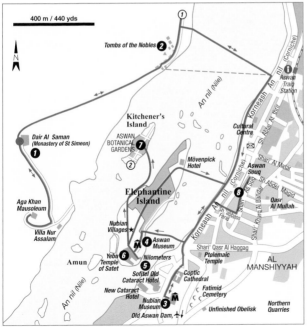

Map labels:

400 m / 440 yds

N

① Aswan Train Station
② Tombs of the Nobles
An nil (Nile)
Kitchener's Island
ASWAN BOTANICAL GARDENS ⑦
Dair Al Saman (Monastery of St Simeon) ❶
Cultural Centre
Korneash An nil (Corniche)
Sh. Abtal Al Tihir
Shari' Al Matar
Aswan Souq
Mövenpick Hotel
Elephantine Island
Aga Khan Mausoleum ❶
Villa Nur Assalam
Nubian Villages ★
Amun
An nil (Nile)
Yebu Temple of Satet ⑥
Aswan Museum ④
Nilometers ⑤
Sofitel Old Cataract Hotel
New Cataract Hotel
Nubian Museum ❸
Coptic Cathedral
Ptolemaic Temple
Shari' Qasr Al Haggag
Sh. abbass Fahir
Korneash An nil (Corniche)
Shari' Al Souq
Sh. Abdel Magid
Shari' Khan Al Bagar
Qasr Al Mullah
AL MANSHIYYAH
Fatimid Cemetery
Unfinished Obelisk
Northern Quarries
Old Aswan Dam

The Nilometer
A vital instrument in Ancient Egypt, the Nilometer *(shown above)* was used to measure the ebb and flow of the Nile, serving both to predict and to record the annual flood – and ensuing harvest. Above 15 cubits (around 0.5m/1½ft), the harvest was predicted to be good; higher, there was the risk of flooding; lower, the risk of famine. Conversely, the better the harvest, the higher the taxes owed to the pharaoh and priesthood by the populace.

south for a closer look at the outside of the single-domed **Aga Khan Mausoleum** (closed to the public). The Ismaili sect's 48th imam, the Aga Khan (who died in 1957) loved to winter at Aswan with his wife, the Begum. Both are buried here. Close by lies their former winter villa, Nur Assalam.

Tombs of the Nobles

Head back northwards towards the ferry jetty. Diagonally opposite, dug into the hillside, are the **Tombs of the Nobles ❷** (daily 8am–4pm, summer to 5pm; charge), accessible via a steep flight of steps.

Belonging to Aswan's former pharaonic rulers, nobles and dignitaries, most of the rock tombs date from the Old and Middle Kingdoms, although those nearest the river are Roman. Dozens honeycomb the hillside, but just five are currently open. Though they bear no comparison in either size or artistry to Luxor's Valley of the Kings, they're still well worth visiting.

The interiors have been badly damaged, but in a few places the original colours remain. Wall carvings testify to victories and punitive raids against the Nubians and trading expeditions to Ethiopia and beyond. Probably the most impressive and best preserved is the 2nd-millennium **Sarambutwan's Tomb** (no. 31), which contains a well-painted niche in the burial chamber depicting the governor with his wife and mother; four decorated columns;

six android (man-shaped) sarcophagi occupying niches along the corridor chamber; and a carved, pink granite offering table.

Miku and Sabny's Tombs (nos 25 and 26), for a father and son who were both governors, date to the 3rd millennium BC and contain nine unusual tapering columns.

The tomb belonging to the governor **Sarambut I** (no. 36) dates to the 2nd millennium BC and has the largest burial chamber, with six decorated pillars and a painted entrance depicting Sarambut and his sons.

Above the tombs is **Qubbet Al Hawa**, the tomb of a local holy man. There's not much here, but the views over the river from this high vantage point are spectacular.

The **Beyt el-Kerem**, see ⑪①, a five-minute walk north of the ferry pier, is a convenient and pleasant place for elevenses, a late breakfast or early lunch. When you're finished, catch a ferry back to the East Bank.

EAST BANK

Nubian Museum

It is around a 30-minute walk from the train station to the **Nubian Museum ❸** (tel: 097-231 9111; daily 9am–9pm; charge); hop in a taxi (around LE10–15) if you are tired. The award-winning museum provides a comprehensive and informative overview of Nubian his-

tory, art, culture and traditions; its design takes its inspiration from traditional Nubian architecture.

Highlights include the spectacular and finely wrought horse armour that dates to the 6th century BC (with captions about grisly Nubian noble burial rituals), silver crowns of Nubian kings, a beautifully fashioned mummy of a ram dedicated to Khnum *(see p.27)*, a lovely ivory-made 'backgammon' set, good dioramas of traditional Nubian life and an interesting model of the mud-brick fortress of Buhen *(c.1875 BC)*.

It's a 15-minute walk from the Nubian Museum to the start of the Corniche, from where you can take a ferry to **Elephantine Island**.

ELEPHANTINE ISLAND

Aswan Museum

The **Aswan Museum** ❹ (tel: 097-230 2066; daily, winter 8am–5pm, summer 8.30am–6pm; charge) lies to the left of the ferry landing on the island's southern tip. It occupies a 19th-century colonial villa that belonged to Sir William Willcocks, the architect of the first Aswan dam.

The main building is home to a dusty, neglected and rather unimaginatively displayed collection of artefacts found in and around Aswan. Highlights are the delightful animal-shaped kohl-grinding plates, the anthropoid sarcophagus, the painted mummy and the ancient Nubian pottery.

The better-organised modern annexe (which dates to 1998) is located down some steps to the right. It houses an eclectic collection of exhibits relating to life on ancient Elephantine, ranging from mummies and sarcophagi to jewellery and weapons, dating from pre-Dynastic times to late Roman.

Nilometers

Below the museum at the water's edge lie two **Nilometers** ❺ (same ticket as museum; *see margin, left*), one dating to the 6th century BC, the other to Ptolemaic times. On the latter, carved Greek, Roman, pharaonic and Arabic numerals serve as a measure on its wall.

Yebu

Spread around the back of the Aswan Museum (and, some would say, much more interesting) are the impressive and atmospheric remains of Aswan's first settlement, the ancient town of **Yebu** ❻ (same ticket and opening

Above from far left: Nubian religious art; feluccas on the Nile.

The Nubian Predicament

Thanks to international efforts coordinated by Unesco, Nubia's most important temples have been saved *(see p.96)*. Unfortunately, Nubia's villages weren't so lucky. Flooding caused by the two dams' construction forced tens of thousands of Nubians to relocate elsewhere, including to Aswan, Kom Umbu, Sudan and Ethiopia, as well as Western countries. Though Nubians were assisted by the Egyptian government in finding new homes, the wholesale upheaval has taken a heavy toll on traditional Nubian society, identity and culture.

Food and Drink 🍴

① BEYT EL-KEREM

North of the Tombs of the Nobles, West Bank; tel: 019-2399 443; £
The Nubian-run Beyt el-Kerem is actually a hotel *(see p.114)*, but it still welcomes travellers at its rooftop restaurant. Food is fresh and well prepared and is served to a backdrop of lovely views over the Tomb of the Nobles, Nubian villages and the Nile.

hours as museum) founded around 3100 BC *(see margin, opposite)*.

The site, currently under investigation by Swiss and German archaeologists, remains little excavated, except for the partly reconstructed Old Kingdom **Temple of Khnum**. Yebu served as a major cult centre to Khnum *(see p.27)*, the god of the annual flooding, right up to the Christian era.

Other ruins of interest include a huge and finely carved granite 'throne', a gateway with carvings of Alexander II praying to Khnum, a Greco-Roman necropolis of Sacred Rams, a small step pyramid attributed to Sneferu (2613–2589 BC) and a large, heavily restored temple dedicated by Hatshepsut (1472–1457 BC) to Setet, the fertility goddess. There's also a 'Panoramic Platform', affording lovely views of the Nile.

The booklet *Elephantine: The Ancient Town,* sold at the museum, is a useful guide.

Nubian Villages

A path leading towards the Mövenpick hotel (unmistakable for its ugly projection resembling an air-traffic-control tower) takes you through a couple of traditional Nubian villages and their gardens. Villagers may invite you in for tea and a tour, or to inspect souvenirs and handicrafts. If you're keen to see hear traditional Nubian music or dance, ask here.

Ancient Nubia

For millennia, Nubia and Egypt were separate territories. Nubia stretched from Aswan to Khartoum, and the First Cataract (a shallow stretch of the Nile) marked the boundary. The Ancient Egyptians called the area Ta-Sety (Land of the Archers) after the Nubian's favoured weapon; their warriors were long known for their prowess in battle, often forming a special force in the pharaoh's army. Nubia was valued above all for its trade routes linking Egypt directly with sub-Saharan Africa, as well as its highly valuable resources including gold, ivory, ebony and copper; Nubia's name derives from the ancient Egyptian word for gold: *nbw*. From around 3100 BC (when Upper and Lower Egypt were united) Nubia was dominated by Egypt, bar just one period when Nubian pharaohs usurped the Egyptian throne (747–656 BC). Many Egyptian pharaohs sent expeditions there and built mud-brick fortresses and temples along the Nile. Look out for the temple and tomb carvings testifying to many bloody battles.

The Mövenpick's ferry sails to the landing on the opposite bank. Both **Panorama** or the cheap and cheerful **Al Masry** *(for both, see p.121)* make excellent late-lunch stops.

ASWAN BOTANICAL GARDENS

Charter a felucca (from LE30 per hour) and sail west towards the northern tip of **Kitchener's Island**, home to **Aswan Botanical Gardens ⑦** (tel: 097-910 1838; daily 7am–5pm, summer to 6pm; charge). Ask your felucca captain to collect you from the southern side of the island, where the shady **Café Kitchener**, see ⑪②, is also found.

The island, measuring 595m/yds by 145m/yds, was presented to Lord Kitchener in the 1890s in return for his services in the Sudan as head of Egypt's forces. A keen amateur botanist with a passion for palms, Kitchener planted the island with an eclectic collection of over 400 species (many labelled), originating from India, Africa and Southeast Asia.

The island, with a small research station and interesting 'Herbarium' – a display on some of the garden's plants and their uses – covers almost 7 hectares (17 acres). With its verdant canopy filled with birds, blossom and scents, and a climate that seems to be cooler by several degrees, it feels like a different world from elsewhere in Aswan.

Paths, lined with benches, circumnavigate and criss-cross the island, affording lovely views of the Nile against a red desert backdrop. Nubian children sometimes approach the island in home-made boats and singing traditional songs.

ASWAN SOUQ

Back on the East Bank, head for the bustle, colour and vibrancy of **Aswan Souq ⑧**, which runs principally along and just off **Shari' As Suq**. Away from the rather touristy main thoroughfare, you can find colourful spice and herb stalls (many still used for traditional medicine), Nubian-made baskets, musical instruments, stuffed or dried animals used as charms and much more. Goods for which Aswan is renowned include *karkadeh* (dried hibiscus flowers), used locally to make hot or cold tea, hand-woven scarves, spices and baskets.

Above from far left:
Aswan Souq.

Ancient City of Yebu
From the earliest pharaonic times up to the early Islamic period, Yebu was a major trade centre. The name means 'ivory', and caravans of camels and elephants laden with ivory, gold, slaves and spices would journey to Yebu from kilometers around. Established initially as a fortress to defend Egypt's southern frontier, it also served as a customs station, later evolving into a trading hub. From here also great pharaonic military and trading expeditions into Nubia, Sudan and Ethiopia were launched.

Food and Drink

② CAFÉ KITCHENER
Aswan Botanical Gardens, Kitchener's Island; daily 8am–5pm, summer to 6pm
Located on the southern tip of Kitchener's Island amid palms and tropical vegetation, the Café Kitchener is a cool, shady and sweet-smelling spot for a drink and much beloved by well-heeled locals. Food is not served.

PHILAE AND THE ASWAN DAMS

Covering all the highlights around Aswan, this half-day tour spans nearly four millennia and explores some of the ancient and modern world's greatest engineering feats. Benefiting from both ancient and modern technical know-how is the evocative and beautifully set Philae Temple.

Lake Nasser

Since its construction, Lake Nasser has helped to avert both flood and famine, increasing the area of cultivable land by 30 percent and doubling the country's electricity generation. More controversially, however, it has submerged thousands of Nubian villages *(see margin, p.81)*, the higher water-table is threatening the monuments along the Nile's banks, and bilharzia incidence has increased. Without the silt, the soil has also become very saline, and farmers are increasingly forced to rely on chemical fertilisers for crop production.

DISTANCE 30km (19 miles) drive round trip
TIME A half-day
START Granite Quarries
END Temple of Isis
POINTS TO NOTE

Cheaper and faster than taking multiple taxis is to hire one for a half-day (c.LE200–250). Ask your hotel to write down the names of the sites you want to visit in Arabic, then negotiate the price before leaving. For Philae, you'll also need to negotiate a 10- to 15-minute boat ride (from LE40 for 1–8 people for a 60- to 90-minute visit). You should also tip the skipper or often a boy working for the captain. Bring lots of water, a sunhat and sunscreen.

Providing great insights into times old and new, Aswan's monuments are important historical records. The unfinished obelisk reveals much about ancient quarrying techniques; the two dams have transformed modern Egypt's fortunes; and, at Philae, one of the Western world's last pagan temples flourished right up until the 4th century AD.

Leaving Aswan south along the Corniche road, look out for the historic **Sofitel Old Cataract Hotel** *(see p.115)*, and, near the quarries, the hundreds of mud-brick domes and tombs of the so-called **Fatimid Cemetery**. Some tombs belong to holy men and date back to the 9th century.

GRANITE QUARRIES AND UNFINISHED OBELISK

Just off the highway about 1.5km (1 mile) from town is what was one of Ancient Egypt's most important **Granite Quarries ❶** (daily, winter 7am–4pm, summer 8am–6pm; charge). Source of the supremely durable pink stone used for Ancient Egypt's monuments, the quarries are like a living workshop that reveal fascinating insights into pharaonic building techniques and technology.

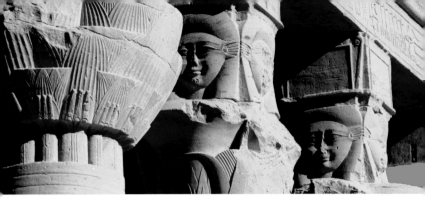

Unfinished Obelisk

The site's highlight is the **Unfinished Obelisk**. Had it not been abandoned after it developed a crack, it would have weighed nearly 1,170 tonnes and become the world's largest standing obelisk. Measuring 41.75m (137ft) high, the obelisk is popularly ascribed to Queen Hatshepsut, but was probably destined to decorate the temple of Thutmose III at Karnak.

Look out for the row of holes chiselled into the block, where wooden wedges were inserted *(see margin, p.28)*. During the annual flooding, the Nile's water would have reached the quarry, facilitating their transportation *(see margin, p.28)*.

THE DAMS

Continue further south past the First Cataract to the **Old Aswan Dam ②**.

Old Aswan Dam

Built by British engineers between 1898–1902, the 50m (164ft) high and 2km (1¼-mile) long dam was at the time the largest in the world. Its 180 sluice gates created a reservoir more than 225km (140 miles) long.

Though the dam was twice raised, it was clear by 1952 that Egypt required a larger dam in order to sustain its burgeoning population. President Nasser *(see margin, p.33)* realised that a new dam positioned 6km (4 miles) further south would boost Egypt's agricultural

and hydroelectrical capacity, making the country more productive and self-reliant. Refused a loan by the World Bank, Nasser controversially turned to the Soviet Union; the original turbines were Soviet-made.

High Dam

The Corniche leads past the Shallal boat dock to Nasser's new dam, known simply as the **High Dam ③**. Just before it, 13km (8 miles) from town is the **Museum of the High Dam** (daily 8.30am–5pm; charge), inside the Visitor Service Centre, where there's also the **High Dam Café**, see ⑪① *(p.87)*. Though currently closed, it should reopen in

Cult of Isis

Wife of Osiris, god of the underworld (whom she magically resurrected after his evil brother, Seth, slayed him and scattered his body parts throughout Egypt), Isis *(see p.26–7)* was goddess of magic and protector of the dead. She was also the mother-goddess, and her cult later spread throughout the Hellenistic and Roman world. The image of the Virgin Mary and Jesus is believed to have evolved directly from the worship of Isis suckling her infant son Horus.

Map:

Qubbet Al Hawa ★
(Al Uqsur) Luxor
Dair Al Saman ★
Aswan
Agha Khan ★ Mausoleum
★ Sidi Harun
1 Granite Quarries & Unfinished Obelisk
Salugah
Northern Quarries
Saheyle
Southern Quarries
Unfinished Sarcophagus
First Cataract
Ash Shallal
★ Unfinished Colossus
Old Aswan Dam **2**
Awd
Agilioqyyah
4 Temple of Isis, Philae
Al Hishah
Bigah
An nil (Nile)
Abu Simbel
2 km / 1¼ miles
Soviet-Egyptian Memorial ★
1 High Dam (Sadd Al 'aali)
3
Hydroelectric Station
Lake Nasser
Terminus of Nile Valley Railway
Temple of Kalabshah, Bayt Al Wali & Qertassi

Above: stone carvings, including *(top)* a Coptic Cross at the Temple of Isis.

High Dam Facts and Statistics
Around 35,000 people laboured on the dam, and 451 men lost their lives in the process. Some 40,000 Nubians required rehousing as a result of its construction.

2012. A 24-minute film about the dam's construction is shown.

Completed in 1971, the dam measures 111m (364ft) high, 3.4km (2 miles) long and 980m (3,215ft) wide, and gave birth to Lake Nasser. Stretching south over 500km (300 miles) all the way into Sudan and covering over 6,000 sq km (2,300 sq miles), Lake Nasser is the second-largest reservoir in the world. Equivalent in mass to 18 Great Pyramids of Khufu, the dam is unquestionably one of the 20th century's great feats of engineering.

TEMPLE OF ISIS, PHILAE

Return on the same road to the Shallal dock for a boat *(see grey Points to Note box, p.84)* to the **Temple of Isis** at **Philae ❶** (Agiliqiyyah Island; daily 7am–4pm, summer to 5pm; charge), some 9km (5 miles) south of Aswan.

Temple Relocation

Originally the Temple of Isis was situated on the island of Philae, which faced Bigah Island. After the first dam was built, Philae was submerged by water for six months of the year, with the High Dam threatening to cause it to keep it that way for good. Therefore, a remarkable joint effort by Unesco and Egypt's Supreme Council of Antiquities relocated the temple to higher grounds, and even landscaped its new home, the nearby island of Agiliqiyyah, to resemble Philae. All

the monuments were meticulously rebuilt stone by stone, according to their original design and layout.

History

For over 800 years right up until AD 550, Philae's temple was one of Egypt's main cult centres. It was dedicated to Isis, who enjoyed a huge cult following. Begun in 289 BC, it was added to by different rulers of the Ptolemaic Dynasty (310–30 BC) and Roman emperors for the next 500 years.

Temple Layout

Boats land in the southwest, near the ancient quay and the **Vestibule of Nectanebo I**, which once formed part of an older temple. Just beyond lies a large temple court lined on both sides by an elegant **colonnade**; note the reliefs of Tiberius making offerings to Egyptian gods on the western columns.

The colonnade leads to the massive **First Pylon** built by Ptolemy II Philadelphos and completed by Ptolemy III Euergetes. The long narrow niches in the pylon once held huge flagpoles. On the right, just inside the pylon's gateway, look out for the inscription in French commemorating the victory in 1799 of General Desaix over the Mamluks.

Inside lies the temple's forecourt with the colonnaded **Priests' Quarters** on the right, and the 3rd-century BC **Birth House** *(see margin, p.90)* on the left. In the furthest (and most northerly) room, look for the fine

relief of Isis suckling her baby in the Delta marshes.

A smaller gate, flanked by two granite lions, leads to the **Second Pylon** and **Pronaos** (hypostyle hall). Here Christian services were celebrated; note the Christian crosses carved on either side of the Second Pylon and elsewhere. The shocking chiselling-out of the carvings (including on the pylon's facades) and the total expunging of Isis' face in the Inner Sanctuary is also the result of over-zealous Christian pagan-purging.

Beyond the hypostyle is the **Inner Sanctuary**. On the pedestal, the sacred barge and gold image of Isis would have gleamed. Stairs lead to the upper floor and the **Osiris Chapel**, where reliefs depict Isis, Horus and Osiris.

West of the temple lies the **Gateway of Hadrian**, beside a ruined vestibule with a stairway leading down to the water. Note also the beautiful carving of Isis watching a crocodile carrying her husband's body to the island of Bigah.

Kiosk of Trajan and Temple of Hathor

Southeast of the complex is the graceful **Kiosk of Trajan**, with its 14 columns and picturesque Nile-side setting. Keep an eye out for the carvings of Trajan offering incense to the gods. To the east lies the **Temple of Hathor**, the goddess of beauty, joy and music. On the colonnade are lively reliefs showing the gods playing instruments and drinking.

The **Philae Café**, see ①②, near the boat landing, provides welcome shade and iced drinks. Philae also has its own Sound and Light Show; check www. soundandlight.com.eg for times.

BACK TO ASWAN

The tour ends at the Temple of Isis, so return to Aswan for lunch and catch a boat from Shallal dock. The **Panoroma** *(see p.121)* on the Corniche enjoys a great riverside setting. If you're at a loose end later, a three-hour round trip by felucca to **Saheylle Island**, 4km (2½ miles) upriver makes a gorgeous jaunt (from LE80 by negotiation). After navigating the mini whirlpools and white water of the **First Cataract**, visit Saheylle's granite boulders (to the south), which are covered with inscriptions thought to date from the 3rd to 20th dynasties, including reference to the great famine of Djoser's reign.

Above from far left: colonnade and First Pylon at the Temple of Isis; view over the High Dam; electric pylons incongruously pepper the Aswan landscape.

Food and Drink 🍴

① HIGH DAM CAFÉ
High Dam; daily 8.30am–5pm
The only café in the vicinity of the dams is the one in the Visitor Service Centre of the High Dam. It's not very characterful or inspiring, but it's friendly and very cheap, selling hot and cold drinks but no food.

② PHILAE CAFÉ
Philae, Agiliqiyyah Island; daily 7am–5pm, summer to 6pm
With tables shaded by parasols and trees set at the very edge of the river, the Philae is a picturesque (albeit pricey) spot for hot or cold drinks or an ice cream. By the end of 2011, the café should also serve food.

PTOLEMAIC TEMPLES

Though less famous that their pharaonic father-temples at Luxor and Karnak, the Ptolemaic temples lying between Aswan and Luxor are no less fascinating. Kom Umbu, Edfu and Esna are home to Egypt's best; scattered at almost equal distances along the Nile, they make for a terrific day trip.

DISTANCE 220km (135 miles)
TIME A full day
START Aswan
END Luxor
POINTS TO NOTE

Restrictions on travel between Aswan and Luxor have been lifted, but check the situation on the ground with your hotel or the tourism office *(see p.107)*. Luxor–Aswan buses and trains stop in Kom Umbu, Edfu and Esna, but you'll need to take taxis or calèches to/from the stations. Simpler and faster is to go on an organised tour (not all stop at Esna) or, better, hire a taxi (from LE450) from Aswan to Luxor via the three temples. Bring a picnic and plenty of water; there are limited dining options en route. After the tour, overnight in Luxor *(see p.113)*.

Above: Kom Umbu.

From Aswan the road follows the river for 20km (12 miles), passing domed tombs and ochre-painted Nubian villages set against a red desert backdrop.

DARAW

After about 43km (27 miles) the road comes to the village of **Daraw ❶**, the site of Egypt's largest **camel market** (Souq Al Gimaal; daily 6.30am–1pm). Try to visit the market before 10.30am, when the trading and bartering is at its liveliest (Sunday is the best day). Many herdsmen and camels walk all the way from Sudan along the Forty Days Road that crosses the desert to a place north of Abu Simbel. From there, they are driven by truck to Daraw, where they are sold then sometimes transported onward all the way to Birqash in Cairo.

KOM UMBU

Some 5km (3 miles) further on, take a left turning at the town of **Kom Umbu ❷**, a key military base and trading hub for gold and elephants in Ptolemaic times. Here, in a superb setting on a promontory above the Nile is the **Temple of Haroeris and Sobek** (daily 7am–5pm, summer to 6pm; charge).

Unusual for being dedicated to two deities, the temple is divided into two

symmetrical halves: the eastern half is dedicated to the crocodile god Sobek, who symbolised strength and ferocity, the western half to Horoeris (Horus the Elder), known as the 'Good Doctor'.

Near the entrance from the river on the left is the **Chapel of Hathor**; peek through the grilles to see piles of mummified crocodiles and their sarcophagi (excavated nearby). Live crocodiles apparently used to swim in a pool near the well on the temple's other side.

A double entrance leads into the inner **hypostyle hall** with its blooming floral columns and vulture-covered ceiling, and on into two symmetrical sanctuaries. Look behind the sanctuaries at the outer walls of the seven **chapels**; carvings depict instruments used to perform brain surgery and dental work – evidence of ancient Egypt's level of medical knowledge and advancement. In the centre of the northern wall is a depiction of Roman emperor and thinker, Marcus Aurelius.

Food and Drink 🍴

① RURAL HOME
Directly below Kom Umbu temple; daily 7am–2am; £
Designed like a traditional village (complete with Bedouin tent, souq, etc) Rural Home clearly targets tourists, but it's well designed using authentic artefacts, charges reasonable prices and has plenty of seating under parasols and cooling air misters. Food options range from pizza to chicken dishes.

If you need refreshment at this point, the **Rural Home**, see 🍴①, is located right below the temple.

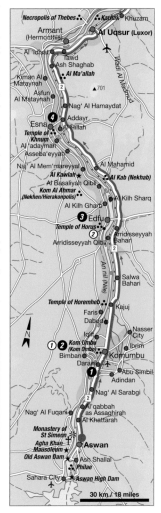

Above from far left: the Temple of Horus, at Edfu; Kom Umbu's Temple of Haroeris and Sobek.

Ptolemaic Temple-Spotting
Though often dressed in the classic pharaonic style (including even their Greek or Roman patrons dressed as phoney-pharaohs complete with cartouches and hieroglyphs), Ptolemaic (c.300 BC–AD 30) temples are given away by a few tell-tale signs: by their 'birth houses' (see margin, p.90), the composite capitals of the columns (often representing different plant motifs such as lotus flowers and papyrus) and the 'Three Bs', as Egyptian guides like to put it: breasts, bottoms and belly buttons – features never represented in real pharaonic art.

Birth Houses

One of the defining features of Ptolemaic temples were the so-called 'birth houses'. Here, in a temple annexe, the annual rituals associated with the birth of the king/deity were performed. These birth houses were a key part of demonstrating the ruler's descent from gods, and thus an entitlement to rule.

Above: falcon statue, Temple of Horus; Temple of Khnum.

EDFU

Return to the main road and continue for 65km (40 miles), past the village of Arridisseyyah Bahari, and cross to **Edfu ❸** on the West Bank. The **Temple of Horus** (tel: 097-471 1716; daily 7am–7pm, summer to 8pm; charge) lies behind the town centre.

Said to mark the site of a epic power struggle between Horus and his wicked uncle, Seth *(see p.27)*, the site was, since ancient times, an important cult centre. The monumental Ptolemaic temple was built between 237–57 BC in the classic Pharaonic style and is one of the finest and best-preserved temples in Egypt. The elaborate carvings have provided Egyptologists with much information on ancient ceremonies.

Guarding the First Pylon are two granite statues of Horus in his falcon form. The carvings inside the walls and up the staircase illustrate the Festival of the 'Beautiful Meeting', in which the statue of Horus was carried to Hathor's temple in Dandarah. The **Birth House** *(see margin, left)* outside the temple has fine carvings of the Ptolemies and the divine birth and suckling of Horus, son of Isis and Osiris *(see p.26)*.

Just past the ticket entrance, there is a café, see ⑪②, where you can get drinks and ice creams.

ESNA

Continue north for 53km (33 miles) to the small town of **Esna ❹**, for centuries an important revitalling point for camel caravans between Sudan and Cairo.

Lying around 200m/yds inland from the quayside on the West Bank is the **Temple of Khnum** (daily 6am–5pm, summer to 6pm; charge), rebuilt by Ptolemy VI (180–145 BC). Once almost certainly as large as Edfu's temple, so far only the temple's forest-like **hypostyle hall** (built by Emperor Claudius in the 1st century AD) has been excavated, revealing 24 columns with different, floral-motifed capitals, many bearing their original colours.

On the walls of the hall from floor to ceiling in beautiful relief, various Roman emperors are seen making offerings to Egyptian deities. Look out also for the Christian crosses and lion-headed font; Esna was once also a flourishing centre of Christianity. Opposite, a couple of tiny cafés serve coffee and tea.

Return to the main road, where the 54km (33½-mile) trip to Luxor takes you through some of the most beautiful and fertile country of the Nile Valley.

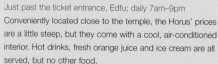

Food and Drink 🍴

② TEMPLE OF HORUS CAFÉ

Just past the ticket entrance, Edfu; daily 7am–9pm
Conveniently located close to the temple, the Horus' prices are a little steep, but they come with a cool, air-conditioned interior. Hot drinks, fresh orange juice and ice cream are all served, but no other food.

ABU SIMBEL

After Giza's pyramids, Abu Simbel's temple is arguably Egypt's most iconic ancient monument. It also epitomises the popular image of the all-conquering pharaoh going to extreme lengths to ensure his own divinity. Amazing travellers for millennia, Rameses' glorious Sun Temple shouldn't be missed.

Situated 277km (172 miles) south of Aswan, just 40km (25 miles) north of the Sudanese border, Abu Simbel lies deep in Ancient Nubia. Built by Rameses II, the great imperialist pharaoh in the 13th century BC, the monuments were clearly meant to impress. Erected following victories against the Nubians among other enemies, the temples would have helped persuade the pharaoh's subjects overwhelmingly of his power and might *(see p.28)*.

Abu Simbel's temples ❶ (daily 6am–5pm, summer to 6pm; separate

DISTANCE 290km (180 miles), one-way from Aswan

TIME A full day

START/END Aswan

POINTS TO NOTE

Security restrictions *(see p.100)* mean that foreigners are currently only permitted to travel in the region by bus in armed convoy. Most opt for an organised tour (with temple admission and guide included), but there's also a local bus (LE25; about 4 hours), which leaves four times daily from the Wadi el-Nil Restaurant on Aswan's main drag (in theory only four foreigner passengers are permitted per bus). Egypt Air (tel: 097-231 5000; www.egyptair.com.eg) flies twice daily to Abu Simbel from Aswan (45-minute round trip, about LE470 including bus transfers to and from the site). Book well in advance. If you overnight in Abu Simbel *(see p.115)*, you can visit the temple in the late afternoon and/or early morning and so avoid the coach crowds.

Temple Cruise

Abu Simbel can also be seen as part of a three-or four-day cruise on Lake Nasser, visiting the lesser-known but equally interesting Nubian temples on the lake's shores *(see p.97)*.

Above from far left: young man at the camel market at Daraw *(see p.88)*; the magnificent Temple of Rameses II at Abu Simbel.

Above from far left:
statues at the Temple
of Rameses II; there
are strict rules
regarding photo-
graphy in order to
protect the temple.

charge for both temples) were 'discovered' in 1812 by the Swiss explorer
Jean-Louis Burckhardt, as he sailed
past them on the Nile. At the time, all
he could see were the colossal heads
sticking out of the sand. Burckhardt
reported the find to the Italian amateur archaeologist Giovanni Belzoni,
who, after five years of fundraising
and excavation, managed to excavate
enough sand from the entrance to slip
inside. He was probably the first to do
so in 2,000 years.

TEMPLE OF RAMESES II

It took 30 years to build the **Temple of
Rameses II**. In 1255 BC, the pharaoh
finally dedicated it to the gods Ra-
Horakhty, Amun-Ra and Ptah *(see
p.26–7)*, but above all to his divine self.

Exterior

Four colossal, 21m (69ft) high seated
figures of Rameses II guard the temple's facade. The torso and head is
missing from the second colossus on
the left, due to it having been toppled by an earthquake in Rameses'
own lifetime; some of the broken
part still lies where it fell, at the foot
of the monument.

Flanking the giant legs are smaller
carvings of Rameses' mother, Queen
Muttuya, his wife Nefertari and some
of his favourite children.

The falcon-headed sun-god Ra-
Horakhty stands in a niche above

the temple door. Set high along the
temple cornice, a row of baboons
worship the rising sun (the temple
faces the east). Gods decorate the
sides of the thrones, while beneath
them are representations of enslaved
Nubians and Hittites.

Hypostyle Hall

The entrance portal leads to a huge
monolithic hypostyle hall containing
eight 10m (33ft) high Osirian colossi
of a youthful-looking Rameses II. The
hypostyle walls are decorated with
dynamic and sometimes bloodthirsty
sunken reliefs of Rameses defeating
his enemies – the Hittites, Libyans and
Nubians – as well as demonstrating his
personal prowess in battle.

On the north wall is the dramatically
depicted Battle of Qadesh (*c.*1274
BC), in what is modern-day Syria.
Look out for the famous depiction of
Rameses multi-tasking – driving his
chariot and shooting arrows at the
same time as his enemies flee.

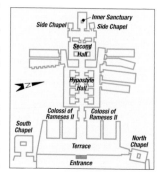

Saving the Temple
With the construction
of the High Dam
threatening to flood
the temple, Unesco
launched a rescue
mission. Costing
£25 million
and involving
archaeologists from
five countries, the
rock-cut temple was
hand-sawn into 1,050
blocks weighing up
to 30 tonnes each,
then reassembled
painstakingly 210m/
yds from the old site,
61m/yds higher up
on an artificial hill. A
remarkable feat, but
one that also puts into
perspective Ramses'
earlier achievement.

Inner Sanctuary

A smaller four-columned vestibule leads to the Inner Sanctuary containing four statues: Ptah, Amun-Ra, Ra-Horakhty and the pharaoh-god Rameses II himself, symbolising Egypt's unity and Rameses' divinity. In front, on the stone pedestal, the sacred barge would have been displayed.

Orientation

More remarkable even than the construction is the temple's orientation. Rameses' architects carefully calculated its position so that at dawn every 21 February and 22 October (the pharaoh's birthday and coronation day), the sun's rays would reach into the Inner Sanctuary and bathe its four deities in light. After relocation *(see margin, left)*, this astonishingly engineered utilisation of a natural phenomenon was nearly replicated; it now happens a day later.

TEMPLE OF HATHOR

To the north of the Temple of Rameses II is the smaller **Temple of Hathor** erected for Rameses' beloved wife Nefertari and dedicated to the cow-goddess Hathor *(see p.26)*. With the rock face flattened to resemble a pylon, six 10m (33ft) high colossi of Rameses and Nefertari stride out of it, while their children stand quietly nearby. Most unusual in temple-building protocol, Nefertari is depicted in equal size to her consort.

Look out for the Hathor-faced capitals of the interior columns and the lovely carvings of the wasp-waisted queen in beautiful, diaphanous robes such as on the east wall of the vestibule to the right of the entrance. On the buttresses on the facade, Rameses' poignant inscription to his queen reads: 'Rameses II, He has constructed a temple, excavated out of the mountain, of eternal craftsmanship, for the Chief Queen, Nefertari, beloved of Mut, in Nubia, for ever and ever, Nefertari for whose sake the sun does shine.'

A good place for refreshments is the **Abu Simbel Temple Coffee Shop**, see ①①, just outside the entrance gates.

If you are sightseeing in the afternoon, you may want to stay on for the Sound and Light Show (www.soundandlight.com.eg; charge), which starts at 7pm in summer, 8pm in winter. Though the script's a bit kitsch and trite, the laser show is done well.

Above: sunken reliefs decorate the walls at the Temple of Rameses II.

Food and Drink

① ABU SIMBEL TEMPLE COFFEE SHOP
Temple Complex entrance gates; tel: 010-257 3991; daily 5am–10pm; £
With lots of seating shaded by trees and cooled by the river, this is a good place for a breather. Service is fast and the menu reasonably wide, with hot and cold drinks, chicken dishes, pizzas, ice cream and biscuits.

LAKE NASSER'S
NUBIAN TEMPLES

A cruise on the Nile is one of the world's most evocative journeys. But opting for Lake Nasser (the river's artificial lake) over stretches of the Nile further north, offers access to much less visited temples, plus the perfect, river-borne arrival at Abu Simbel's marvellous Sun Temple.

DISTANCE 300km (185 miles)

TIME Three nights/four days

START New Kalabashah

END Abu Simbel

POINTS TO NOTE

All but one of the temples can be reached by car, but only on an organised expedition with armed police escort, guide and all provisions including extra petrol (travel agencies can arrange this), which is expensive. A full-board cruise is the easiest, most comfortable way of visiting the temples, though they take a minimum of three nights and four days and vary from the mid-range to the luxurious; there are currently no budget options. Recommended are Mövenpick's *Prince Abbas* (tel: 097-231 4660; www.moevenpick-hotels.com) with excellent facilities, service and food, and the beautifully designed *Kasr Ibrim* and *Eugénie* of Belle Epoque Travel (tel: 02-2516 9655; www.kasribrim.com.eg).

Nile Facts

The world's longest river, the Nile travels 6,680km (4,150 miles) through nine African countries. Since pharaonic times right up to the late 19th century, the Nile's source was one of the great geographical mysteries. In fact, there are two sources: the White Nile in Uganda and the Blue Nile in Ethiopia; the two join together in Khartoum, Sudan. With its almost non-existent rainfall, Egypt would simply not exist without the life-giving water of the great river.

South of Aswan lay the land of Ancient Nubia, which at different times was a vassal state, rival kingdom and even overlord to Ancient Egypt. Royal tombs and temples lined the banks of the 'Nubian Nile' in the south, just as they did in the north. With the construction of Aswan's High Dam in 1971, however, along with the creation of Lake Nasser, more than 6,000 sq km (2,300 sq miles) of the ancient land was submerged, and, with it, many of its ancient sites.

Following a remarkable international rescue operation *(see feature, p.96)*, Nubia's most important temples were salvaged. Relocated, they now occupy four new sites: New Kalabashah, New Subu' (also known as Wadi As Subu'), New Amadah, and Abu Simbel *(see also p.91)*, located in the far south and the best known of the Nubian temples.

NEW KALABASHAH

Lying just south of the High Dam (and visible from it), around 45km (30 miles) north of its original location is **New Kalabashah ❶**.

Temple of Kalabashah

The site of a temple since at least Amenhotep II's time (around 1400 BC), the present **Temple of Kalabashah** dates to Ptolemaic and Roman times and was completed by Augustus in the 1st century BC. The largest of the stone-built Nubian temples, it is grand in scale and well preserved: a large pylon leads into the court and hypostyle hall, and decoration includes fine bas reliefs of the Emperor Augustus making offerings to the gods and three inscriptions, two in Greek, the other in Meroitic (an Ancient Nubian language). In the 6th century, the temple served as a church.

Temple of Bayt Al Wali

The **Temple of Bayt Al Wali** was constructed by Rameses II. Bar the brick-made first pylon in front, the temple was carved into the rock. Note, on the north and south walls of the forecourt, the beautifully carved and coloured reliefs of Rameses' campaigns against the ancient Nubians, Libyans and Syrians.

Temple of Qertassi

Little remains of the Ptolemaic **Temple of Qertassi**, which lies to the north of Kalabashah. Of particular interest here is one hall containing four columns in the Ptolemaic style (with floral-motif capitals), and two 'Hathoric' columns (with capitals featuring the cow-headed goddess) framing the portal.

NEW SUBU'

Next stop is New Subu', home to three temples: Dakkah, Muharraqah and Wadi As Subu' (the last-named is the original, which previously stood at Subu').

Wadi As Subu' Temple

Named 'Valley of the Lions' after the avenue of lion-headed sphinxes, **Wadi As Subu' Temple ❷** was built by Rameses II. It originally lay around 4.5km (2¾ miles) east of its present location. In the courtyard are human-headed sphinxes and in the second court, falcon-headed sphinxes. The temple is

Above from far left: the Temple of Amadah (see p.96); crossing the lake to reach the temples.

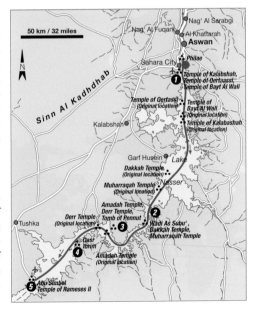

decorated with bas-reliefs of religious and triumphal scenes featuring Rameses and the gods. Just one of the four original colossi of Rameses remain.

Temple of Dakkah

This temple, built by the Meriotic king Arkamani in the 3rd century BC and later enlarged by the Emperor Augustus, is unique for its orientation parallel to the Nile. Ptolemaic in style, it has bas-reliefs showing offerings being made to the gods. The original temple lay 40km (25 miles) north of here.

Temple of Muharraqah

Relocated from a spot around 53km (33 miles) to the north, the diminutive

Above: tourist and guide at Lake Nasser; rowing on the lake.

Temple of Muharraqah was begun under the Emperor Augustus but was never finished, which may explain its lack of any wall decoration. It is the only Ancient Egyptian monument, however, to have a spiral staircase. It later served as a church.

NEW AMADAH

New Amadah is also home to two temples: Amadah and Derr, and the Tomb of Pennut.

Temple of Amadah

Built by Thutmose II, his son Amenhotep II and Thutmose IV (1503–1389 BC), the **Temple of Amadah ❸** is the oldest Nubian temple. It was originally located on a bend in the Nile, where the river briefly flowed southwards before resuming its northerly course. During the 1960s, the French removed it wholesale from the site *(see feature, left)* and transported it on a specially built railway to its new site 2.5km (1½ miles) to the north. Wall carvings show the pharaohs and gods taking part in various religious ceremonies.

Temple of Derr

Originally located 11km (7 miles) south of its present site, the **Temple of Derr** was the only Nubian temple located on the eastern bank. Built by Rameses II to commemorate 30 years of rule, it resembles the Sun Temple of Abu Simbel in design and decoration, but on a much

Saving Ancient Nubia

As the construction of the High Dam neared its completion, the race was on to save the temples. Launched in 1960, the Egyptian-led, Unesco-funded campaign involved over 50 countries, who combined expertise, equipment and funding to excavate ancient sites and salvage 14 temples. Ten of the temples were dismantled then reconstructed piece by piece at new locations above the nascent lake's water level. Four further temples were gifted in their entirety by the Egyptian government to the countries lending most assistance: the Temple of Dabod to Spain (now in Madrid's Parque del Oeste); the Temple of Dendur to the US (now in New York's Metropolitan Museum); the Chapel of Thuthmose III at Al Lesiya to Italy (now in Turin's Egyptian Museum); the Temple of Taffa to Holland (now in the Rijksmuseum, Leiden) and the Ptolemaic Gateway from the Temple of Kalabashah, to the Germans, now in the Egyptian Museum, Berlin.

smaller scale. Look for the painting of Rameses on the north wall of the hall, in which he stands under the sacred *ishad* tree, while the god Thoth records his name on the tree.

Tomb of Pennut

Relocated from a site about 40km (25 miles) south of its current location, the **Tomb of Pennut** was the only Nubian tomb that was rescued by Unesco. The tomb's namesake, Pennut, was an official serving under Rameses VI (*c*.1140–1130 BC). Simple in structure, it consists of an offering hall and burial chamber. Wall paintings depict Pennut during his life and also in the underworld.

QASR IBRIM

Occupying what was once a promontory on the East Bank, the old fortress of **Qasr Ibrim ❹** today stands on an island, and is the only monument of Lake Nasser that occupies its original position. The site dates back to Amenhotep I (*c*.1546 BC), but the surviving building in fact dates to the 7th century and comprises the remains of a Coptic cathedral, the seat of an important bishopric. Later, in the 16th century, the site was used as an Ottoman fort. One of the pharaonic shrines found here has been relocated to Aswan's Nubian Museum *(see p.80)*. Qasr Ibrim is currently closed to the public while excavations are carried out, but cruise boats moor close by for photographs.

ABU SIMBEL

Much the most famous of the Nubian temples, and providing a fitting climax and finale to the monuments to the north, are the awe-inspiring temples of Rameses II at **Abu Simbel ❺** *(see p.91)*. The approach by boat is spectacular and showcases the temples as originally intended: from afar and from the river.

Above from far left: guide explaining the wall paintings at the Temple of Amadah; taking a cruise is the easiest and most comfortable way to visit the sights on Lake Nasser; Temple of Kalabashah *(see p.95)*.

Life on Lake Nasser
Teeming with fish, Lake Nasser yields over 50,000 tonnes annually to local fishermen. The lake is also home to more than 200,000 birds, including migratory species overwintering here. Wildlife to look out for that isn't too uncommon includes the Egyptian goose, the dorca gazelle and the Nile crocodile, which grows to over 2.5m (8ft) long.

Left: relaxing after temple visits at sunset.

DIRECTORY

A user-friendly alphabetical listing of practical information, plus hand-picked hotels and restaurants, clearly organised by area, to suit all budgets and tastes. Select nightlife listings are also included here.

A

AGE RESTRICTIONS

The age of consent in Egypt is 18, which is also the age for the legal purchase of alcohol, and driving with a valid licence.

B

BUDGETING

Egypt is an inexpensive destination. You can expect to stay in a quality three-star hotel, feed yourself on three filling meals and travel for LE400 per day or less. However, admission to the major sights such as the pyramids can add as much as LE500 to your daily budget. If you're a student, don't forget your ISIC card (which usually entitles you to discounts of around 50 percent).

The following gives an idea of average costs; prices are in Egyptian pounds (LE):

Glass of beer: LE7
Bottle of house wine: LE45
Main course at a budget/moderate/ expensive restaurant: LE2–5/10–20/ 30–50
Double room in a budget/moderate/ de-luxe hotel: LE125–175/300–500/ 1,000–3000
Taxi journey to/from airport and downtown Cairo: LE40
Single bus ticket: LE0.50–2
Single metro ticket (Cairo): LE1

C

CHILDREN

Babysitting services are available in many of the upper-range hotels. Children under the age of six are usually admitted to sites for free; from six to 16, and students holding ISIC cards, are entitled to 50 percent discounts.

CLOTHING

Light cotton clothes are suitable for all seasons, but bring a few light jumpers in winter particularly for night-time, when the temperature can plummet. *See also Climate, p.11.*

Egypt is still a traditional and conservative society, and, if travelling independently, you will feel more at ease dressed modestly: avoid transparent and very tight clothing, revealing necklines, shorts or vests (shoulders should ideally be covered). In mosques, clothing should be particularly conservative, and women are usually required to wear headscarves.

CRIME AND SAFETY

Overall, Egypt is a pretty safe place (considerably safer statistically than most Western cities). However, and again as in the US and Europe, the country has been troubled in recent decades by terrorist violence. You can check the latest warnings at your government's

travel advice website (in the UK: www.fco.gov.uk/en/travelling-and-living-overseas/travel-advice-by-country). *See also Religion, p.106.* As a result, the Egyptian government – which depends on tourism as a vital revenue-earner – has greatly tightened security in all the major tourist sights.

Social restrictions on young people in Egypt, and television-fed misconceptions of foreign women, can lead to women travellers attracting a fair amount of attention. It's best ignored. If seriously hassled, ask for help from the white-uniformed tourist police.

CUSTOMS

Duty-free allowances per person are: 1 litre of liquor, 2 litres of wine, 200 cigarettes or 50 cigars or 250 grams of tobacco, and 1 litre of perfume.

Video cameras and computers should be declared on a 'D-form' upon arrival. Ensure any losses are reported to the police, or a 100 percent duty may be levied upon departure.

To protect antiques, Egyptian-made items over 100 years old are not permitted to leave the country without an export permit (obtainable from the Department of Antiquities), nor are foreign-made items deemed to have 'historic value'. Travellers may also be asked to show receipts as proof of payment for valuable items.

Visitors can bring a maximum of LE1,000 into or out of Egypt at any

single time. When exchanging money, keep the receipt; you may be asked for bank receipts when changing Egyptian pounds back into your currency (which is possible at the international airport).

D

DISABLED TRAVELLERS

Currently few public buildings provide facilities for the infirm or disabled, though things are changing slowly. Most of the monuments, however, except the pyramids, some tombs and Philae Temple, are accessible. For more information, see www.egyptforall.com.

E

ELECTRICITY

The power supply is 220 volts. Sockets require a European two-pin plug.

EMBASSIES AND CONSULATES (IN CAIRO)

Australia: World Trade Center, 11th floor, 1191 Corniche An Nil, Bulak; tel: 02-2575 0444; www.egypt.embassy.gov.au

Canada: 26 Shari' Kamel Al Shenawy, Garden City; tel: 02-2791 8700; www.canadainternational.gc.ca/egypt

Ireland: 7th floor, 3 Shari' Abu Al Feda, Zamalek; tel: 02-2735 8264; www.dfa.ie/home/index.aspx?id=5464

Above from far left: on Alexandria's Corniche; boats on the Nile.

Carbon-Offsetting
Air travel produces a huge amount of carbon dioxide and is a significant contributor to global warming. If you want to offset the damage caused to the environment by your flight, a number of organisations can do this for you, using online 'carbon calculators', which tell you how much you need to donate. In the UK travellers can vist www.climatecare.org or www.carbonneutral.com; in the US, log onto www.climatefriendly.com or www.sustainabletravel international.org.

Further Reading: Non-Fiction

• *Alexandria, City of Memory* by Michael Haag (Yale University Press, 2004). Evocative work detailing literary Alexandria.
• *Egypt through Writers' Eyes* edited by Deborah Manley and Sahar Abdel-Hakim (Eland, 2008). Insightful collection of writings about Egypt, its culture and history.
• *A Thousand Miles up the Nile* by Amelia Edwards (Parkway). Lively account of a journey up the Nile in 19th-century style.
• *Cairo: the City Victorious* by Max Rodenbeck (Picador, 1998). Wonderfully written history of Cairo by a long-time resident and aficionado.

UK: 7 Shariʿ Ahmed Ragheb, Garden City; tel: 02-2794 6000; http://ukinegypt.fco.gov.uk/en
US: 8 Kamal Al Din Salah Street, Garden City; tel: 02-2797 3300; http://cairo.usembassy.gov/

EMERGENCY NUMBERS

Ambulance: 123
Fire brigade: 125
Police services: 122
Tourist police: 126

G

GAY/LESBIAN ISSUES

Homosexuality isn't illegal in Egypt, but is taboo and forbidden in the Qur'an. Prosecutions – under the guise of other social order laws – do occur. Despite this, there is underground activity.

GREEN ISSUES

As in many developing nations, environmental concerns do not take top priority in Egypt. The damage caused to the coastline and coral reefs by tourism developments along the Red Sea and Sinai Coast is well documented. Destructive building practice continues apace, though a few eco-lodges are beginning to open in Egypt (notably in Sinai and Siwa), and joint Egyptian-international initiatives are introducing guidelines for greener development.

H

HEALTH

The heat is probably the biggest health hazard in Egypt; a high-factor sunscreen or sunblock is essential. Avoid dehydration (a real danger in the sun) by drinking plenty of fluids.

Though tap water is drinkable in the big cities, it's advisable to stick to the widely available and cheap, bottled mineral water. In addition, it's best to avoid ice cubes in drinks, raw salads and unpeeled fruit.

Insurance
Travel insurance is essential. Check carefully that it includes any activities you plan to do, such as diving, horse-riding, balloon rides, etc.

Hospitals
Well-equipped hospitals are found throughout Egypt, and particularly in Cairo and Alexandria. Cash deposits are usually required to cover the cost of treatment. Keep all receipts and medical bills for reimbursement when you get home.
Anglo-American Hospital Zohoreya, next to the Cairo Tower, Zamalek; tel: 02-2735 6162.
Alternatively, for a list of recommended doctors, dentists, clinics and hospitals (where your home language is usually spoken), ask at your embassy or consulate in Cairo *(see p.101)*.

Pharmacies

Most towns have one or more pharmacies that open from 10am to 10pm (and at least one that will open all night). Egyptian pharmacists usually speak good English and can advise on treatment for a range of ailments. Medicines are generally inexpensive.

A 24-hour pharmacy in Cairo with outlets across the city and that can also arrange delivery to major hotels is Ali and Ali, tel: 02-2760 4277.

Vaccinations

Evidence of yellow fever and cholera immunisation are required from persons who have visited an infected area up to six days prior to arrival.

No other inoculations are officially required, but it's always sensible to be up to date with polio, tetanus and cholera. Rabies is common. If you are bitten by an animal, it's wise to seek health advice immediately.

HOURS AND HOLIDAYS

Opening Hours

Banks: Sun–Thur 8.30am–1.30pm, closed Fri and Sat. Banks at the airport are open 24 hours.

Museums/Monuments: in general these are open 9am–4/5pm, although many close for prayers on Friday 11am–1.30pm.

Shops: Sun–Thur 9am–1pm and 5–9/10pm (winter to 6pm). Some shops also close on Sunday.

Offices: 8am–2pm, closed Friday, and sometimes Saturday or Sunday also. See also 'Post', p.105.

During Ramadan everything opens at least an hour later and closes an hour or two earlier, but shops and some offices reopen 8–10pm.

Public Holidays

1 Jan New Year's Day
25 Apr Sinai Liberation Day
1 May Labour Day
23 July Revolution Day
6 Oct Armed Forces Day
23 Oct Suez Day
23 Dec Victory Day

Religious Holidays

Egypt observes the traditional feast days of the Muslim calendar, including Moulid An Nabi (the Prophet Muhammad's birthday), Ras As Sanaa (Islamic New Year), Ramadan (the month of fasting), Aid Al Fitr (the end of Ramadan), and the Aid Al Kebir, three days of celebrations in commemoration of Abraham's sacrifice of the lamb.

The Muslim feasts depend on the lunar calendar, which shifts backwards by 11 days a year.

Coptic businesses close on 7 January for Coptic Christmas and for Coptic Easter in March or April. The first Monday after Coptic Easter, known as Sham An Nasim ('the smell of the breeze') is celebrated by all Egyptians.

Further Reading: Fiction

- *The Alexandria Quartet* by Lawrence Durrell (Faber, 1962). A classic novel set in Alexandria during the late 1930s and early 1940s.
- *Cairo, A Graphic Novel* by G. Willow Wilson and M.K. Perker (DC Comics NY, 2007). A magic-realist novel.
- *The Cairo Trilogy* by Nobel Prize-winning author Naguib Mahfouz (AUC Press, 1956–7). A family living in Cairo's Old City.
- *Map of Love* by Ahdaf Soueif (Bloomsbury, 2000). An Egyptian novel about a love affair that develops between an American and an Egyptian.
- *The Yaqoubian Building* by Alaa Al Aswany (Fourth Estate, 2007). International best-seller giving fascinating insights into Egyptian society.

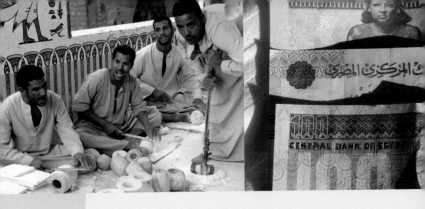

I

INTERNET FACILITIES

The Internet is widely accessible in Egypt. Most hotels now have Wi-Fi (often free in the budget to mid-range hotels; chargeable in the top-range ones). Internet cafés are ubiquitous throughout Egyptian towns, and you shouldn't have too much trouble locating one.

L

LANGUAGE

Arabic is Egypt's official language. Though basic English is widely spoken in tourism areas, it's well worth learning a few words of Arabic. See the inside back flap of the cover for useful words and phrases.

LEFT LUGGAGE

Left-luggage facilities are found at Cairo's international airport and at train stations in Cairo and Luxor.

M

MAPS

Most maps distributed by tourist offices are of poor quality; those sold in Egyptian bookshops (particularly Cairo) are much better.

If driving in Egypt, you may want to purchase a decent-quality road map before arriving.

MEDIA

Newspapers and Magazines

In Cairo, most major European and US newspapers and magazines are available at larger hotels, as well as at newsstands in affluent areas of Cairo such as Zamalek and Maadi, usually a day or more old.

Locally, the two most important dailies are *Al Ahram* (Egypt's oldest paper, founded in 1875, also with an English edition) and *Al Akhbar*.

Decent-quality English-language weeklies include the *Middle East Times* (www.metimes.com) and the *Arab Times.*

Radio

The BBC World Service broadcasts to Egypt on 639 kHz and 1323 kHz (the latter providing better reception between sunrise and sunset). News is on the hour.

The VOA (Voice of America) broadcasts on a variety of wavelengths 3–10am daily, on 1290 Khz.

Television

The majority of hotels offer satellite television with channels available including BBC World and CNN. Local television is usually dominated by Egyptian soap operas and action

movies. See the *Egyptian Gazette* for detailed schedules.

MONEY

Cash Machines

A growing number of towns in Egypt now have ATM machines, though foreign banks usually levy a fairly steep fee for cash withdrawal abroad using debit and credit cards.

Credit Cards

Credit cards are accepted by most mid- to top-end hotels, top-end restaurants and many (though not all) tourist shops, but rarely by shops in the souqs.

Currency

The Egyptian pound (LE), *guineh* in Arabic, is divided into 100 piastres (PT), *irsh* in Arabic. There are notes for 25 and 50 piastres, and 1, 5, 10, 20, 50, 100 and 200 pounds; there are coins of 10, 20 and 25 piastres.

Money Exchange

Exchange bureaux often offer a cheaper and faster way to exchange currency, but check rates and commission first; hotels generally offer the least favourable rates. You can buy and sell Egyptian pounds outside Egypt, but the rate is usually considerably less favourable than when buying or selling Egyptian pounds in Egypt itself.

P

POLICE

Egypt is unusual in having two police forces: the civil police (who usually wear an all-black uniform) and the tourism police (usually clad in white). Neither force has officers who speak much English, but they do usually try to help.

See also Emergency Numbers, p.102.

POST

Egypt Post (tel: 0800-800 2800; www.egypt.post.org), the country's state-owned postal service, covers most of the country and is reasonably efficient. Airmail takes up to seven days to Europe and up to 14 days to the US.

Stamps are available at post offices, souvenir shops and in hotel newsagents. Stamps for both postcards and airmail letter cost LE5 (roughly £0.60 or US$1 at time of printing) to Europe and the US. Mailboxes on street corners and outside post offices are red for regular Egyptian mail, blue for overseas airmail letters and green for Cairo and express mail within Cairo.

Cairo's Central Post Office is at Meadan Al Ataba and is open Sat–Thur 7am–7pm, Friday and public holidays 7am–noon. All other post offices are open 8.30am–3pm daily, except Friday.

Above from far left: workers at an alabaster factory on Luxor's West Bank; Egyptian pounds; some signs are translated into English, too, to help non-Arabic-speaking tourists.

Manners and Etiquette
• Displays of public affection between men and women are frowned upon, though friends of the same sex often hold hands, hug and kiss.
• If you want to photograph people, it's polite to ask first. Always ask women and be prepared for them to say no. *See also Eating Etiquette, p.17, and Mosque Etiquette, p.106.*

Most Egyptian mosques are open to non-Muslims, though some are not. If in doubt, ask locally. Avoid visiting during prayer time (five times a day including noon, mid-afternoon and sunset), when the mosque will be filled with worshippers. The larger mosques have separate entrances for men and women, and you will be politely directed to the appropriate portal. Be sure to dress respectfully when visiting mosques; in many it is preferred that women wear headscarves – these are often provided, along with loose gowns, on site, in return for a tip. Shoes are always removed upon entering a mosque (though shoe covers are sometimes provided as well).

R

RELIGION

Islam is the official religion and the faith of the vast majority of the population, though Egypt is also home to some Christians (especially Copts) and even a small Jewish community.

Coptic Orthodox

The Copts make up around 10 percent of the population. A Christian sect, they separated from the Byzantine and Latin churches in AD 451 over a disagreement in religious doctrine. Copts founded the world's first monasteries, and the monastic tradition continues to form an important part of the Coptic faith *(see p.59)*.

Coptic services are open to all visitors. One of the best places in Egypt to attend a Coptic mass is at Cairo's famous 'Hanging Church' *(see p.57)*.

Religious Tolerance

Prior to independence in 1952, Egypt was a melting pot of cultures and largely tolerant of differing faiths.

Multiple wars against Israel combined with unpopular Western intervention in the wider region has propelled the country towards the religious right, resulting in the upheavals in Middle Egypt that plagued the 1990s.

The government is determined to continue to steer the nation along a path of secularism and tries to ensure religious extremism is kept in check. However, general anti-Western sentiment, unpopular wars in Iraq and Afghanistan and soaring inflation do much to drive youth towards fanaticism, as it does in the wider region.

T

TELEPHONES

Dialling Codes

National: International Dialling Code for Egypt: +20 followed by the local area code (minus the zero).

Local:
Alexandria: 03
Aswan: 097
Cairo: 02
Luxor: 095
General enquiries: 140

International: dial 00 followed by the national code (eg 44 for the UK, 1 for the US and Canada, 61 for Australia, and 353 for Ireland).

Mobile (Cell) Phones

Mobile communication is easy and inexpensive in Egypt. SIM cards are easily purchased, and network charges are surprisingly good value (even to call overseas).

Two mobile phone companies currently providing services on Egypt's GSM system are: MobiNil (tel:

02-760 9090; www.mobinil.com) and Vodaphone (tel: 02-529 2000; vodaphone.com.eg).

Prepaid cards (usually from LE10–300) are widely sold in retail outlets including electronic and telephone shops across the country. They usually expire after 30 days.

TIME ZONES

Egypt is two hours ahead of GMT and observes summer time from 1 May–30 September.

TOURIST INFORMATION

Egypt's international tourist offices are well run and helpful. The government website, www.egypt.travel, is also a useful resource for holiday planning.

Within Egypt, the tourism offices are less useful. Basic questions can be answered but little more.

London

Egyptian Tourism and Information Centre, 3rd floor, Egyptian House, 170 Piccadilly, London W1J 9EJ; tel: 020-7493 5283; email: egypt@ freenetname.co.uk.

Egypt

Alexandria: 23 East Port, Saad Zaghlool Square; tel: 03-484 3380.
Aswan: Meadan Al Mahatta (next to the train station); tel: 097-231 2811 or 097-231 2811.

Cairo: 5 Shari' Adly, Downtown; tel: 02-2391 3454.
Luxor: opposite the Winter Palace, Corniche An Nil; tel: 095-237 3294.

TOURS

Operating since 1979, with offices throughout Egypt and offering multi-lingual staff and guides, is the accommodating Soliman Travel (www.solimantravel.co.uk), an Egyptian-owned tour agency and flight consolidator. Services range from flight bookings and cruises to tailor-made tours and car and driver hire. Offices include:
• **Soliman Travel:** 113 Earls Court Road, London SW5 9RL; tel: 020-7835 1568.
• **Soliman Travel Egypt:** 95 Shari' Faried Semeka, Heliopolis, Cairo; tel: +20 (0)2-635 0350.

TRANSPORT – GETTING THERE

By Air

Egypt's Nile region is served by international airports at Alexandria, Cairo, Aswan and Luxor. Egypt's excellent national airline, Egypt Air (www.egyptair.com.eg), operates daily flights to Cairo from London Heathrow, most European capitals, the US, Canada and Australia, as well as weekly flights from a number of European cities to Luxor.

Cheap Flights
Note that you can get good discounts on domestic flights in Egypt if you buy an international Egypt Air ticket and then book from abroad.

Travelling by Road

Since the terrorist attacks on tourists in the 1990s, travel along parts of the Nile Valley – in particular between Cairo and Luxor, and Aswan and Abu Simbel – has been prohibited to foreigners. In 2009, restrictions on all travel between Luxor and Abydos were lifted (but remain in place further north), but the armed convoy stipulations between Aswan and Abu Simbel are still in force. Vehicles (including buses, taxis, private and hired vehicles) must travel in armed convoy.

All airports are served by taxis and limousines; in Cairo, the new yellow/orange-and-blue taxis (tel: 16516) offer air-conditioning and functioning meters.

In Cairo, the Airport Bus Service (No. 356) operates from Terminal 1, stopping at Meadan At Tahrir in downtown Cairo. Faster and more convenient is the new Airport Shuttle Bus, which runs directly to destinations throughout the city, including Giza, Heliopolis, Zamalek and the downtown area.

By Road

Though private vehicles are not allowed to enter Egypt from Israel, regular buses run to Cairo from Tel Aviv, Jerusalem and Eilat in Israel. Buses and taxis also run between Cairo and Alexandria and Benghazi or Tripoli in Libya.

By Sea

There are no longer any direct ferries from Europe to Egypt. A weekly ferry sails from Wadi Halfa in Sudan up Lake Nasser to Aswan (contact the Nile Navigation Company in Aswan, tel: 097-203-3348).

TRANSPORT – GETTING AROUND

By Air

Egypt Air and its subsidiary Egypt Air Express connect Cairo, Alexandria, Luxor and Aswan, among other places, with regular and reliable flights.

By Bus

Buses connect most cities to Cairo and Alexandria. They range in quality (and price). Buses are best booked the day before. Most inter-city buses now leave Cairo from the Turgoman station, 900m/yds west of Rameses station, on Shari' Al Gisr in Bulak.

By Car

To hire a car, drivers need to be 25 years old and carry an International Driving Licence. Car-hire companies can be found at airports and major hotels. Credit cards are accepted.

Road Rules: road rules and signs are similar to those used in Europe. Cars drive on the right-hand side of the road. Speed limits (often enforced by radar) are posted on major highways and are: motorways 100kph (62mph); other roads 90kph (56mph); and in towns 50kph (30mph).

Road Conditions: the western shore of the Nile serves as the main Cairo–Upper Egypt thoroughfare and is the most congested and dangerous in Egypt.

Driving at night is best avoided.

By Metro and Tram

In Cairo, the metro system is identified by circular signs with a big red 'M'. Clean, cheap and efficient, it's a great way to get around. The first carriage of every train is reserved for

women, who should sit here if travelling alone or in female-only groups; women accompanied by men can sit in the other carriages.

By Rail

The Egyptian State Railway serves the entire Nile Valley from Alexandria (via Cairo) south to Aswan. Trains run every few hours on major routes (though travel for foreigners is restricted in places). Fares are inexpensive compared to those in Europe.

The privately owned Wagon-Lits also operates a (more expensive) sleeper service from Cairo to Luxor (10 hours) and Aswan (15 hours), and several fast and comfortable trains a day to Alexandria. All tickets need to be booked in advance at Rameses station, Cairo, or at Alexandria station.

By Service Taxi

Faster than the buses (though costing about the same and serving similar routes, with several departures daily) are service taxis. Known locally as 'beejous' (from Peugeot, their make), they seat six or seven and leave as soon as they are full. The service taxi station is usually found beside the bus or train station.

By Taxi

Taxis are identified by their orange number plates. Meters are seldom used except in Cairo's fleet of pre-bookable yellow/orange-and-blue taxis.

Always agree a fare before getting into non-metered taxis. Most taxi drivers are honest, but will often quote higher fares to foreigners. Ask your hotel for an estimated fare before departing and make sure you carry small change and notes to pay for it.

Fares usually cost around LE5–10 for short 10–15-minute journeys, LE15–20 for longer ones, LE50 for long distances such as from town to Cairo airport, and LE150–200 to hire per day within Cairo.

V

VISAS AND PASSPORTS

All visitors to Egypt must hold passports valid for a minimum of six months. Almost all Europeans, North Americans, Australians and New Zealanders must obtain a tourist visa. These can be obtained usually in a few days from Egyptian consulates abroad (for up to three months' validity), but one-month, single-entry tourist visas are also issued on the spot upon arrival at Cairo or Luxor airport (but not at the Israeli border).

Visas can be extended at the Mugama'a (Cairo's central administrative building on Meadan At Tahrir). You normally have a 15-day grace period after the expiry date, but if you don't renew it, you'll be liable for a fine and will need to obtain a formal letter of apology from your embassy.

Above from far left: navigating the Nile; herders and their charges.

Women Travellers
There's a simple rule of thumb: the more conservatively you dress *(see also Clothing, p.100)*, the less hassle and fewer comments and suitors you will attract. Though comments such as *helwa* ('sweet' or 'beautiful') are common, as is the occasional touch, serious physical harassment is very rare. If harassed, ask a policeman, shopkeeper or passerby for help.

ACCOMMODATION

Hotels on the Nile run the gamut from flea-pit to pharaoh's folly and everything in between. Generally, they represent good value for money, but beware of relying on Egypt's star-rating system. The country's biggest problem is maintenance: a hotel rated five stars 10 years ago may not deserve three today. In Cairo, with ever-increasing competition, hotels are finally undergoing some renovation. In Luxor and Aswan, however, the stars burn less bright. Check out recent travellers' reports on the Internet.

For mid- to low-range options, however, accommodation in towns and cities along the Nile is a bargain, particularly during the low season. Research web deals; online prices are often lower than those quoted by phone or at the hotels themselves. Be sure to book well in advance in the high season, especially for Aswan and Abu Simbel.

Beware of hotel scams. Taxi drivers may try to take you elsewhere for commission. If you arrive without reservations, head for the tourism office, which will give impartial advice.

Price for a standard double room for one night, including taxes and breakfast, during peak season:

££££	over £65
£££	£25–65
££	£10–25
£	under £10

Cairo

Carlton Hotel

21 Shari' 26 July, Downtown (near the Cinema Rivoli); tel: 02-2575 5181; www.carltonhotelcairo.com; £–££

With its wood panelling, spaciousness and ceiling fans, the Carlton has an Old-World feel. Well maintained and well run, it boasts a restaurant and pleasant rooftop café/bar. Room rates vary according to size and decor but prices include half-board. Centrally located and comfortable, it represents outstanding value for money.

Longchamps Hotel

21 Shari' Ismail Muhammad, Zamalik; tel: 02-2735 2311; www.hotellongchamps.com; ££

A well-kept secret among those who visit Cairo often, the Longchamps feels more like a Parisian private house than a hotel, and is well managed by the helpful Heba Bakri and her husband Chris. Rooms are spotless and many have balconies overlooking the leafy streets of Zamalik. A good buffet breakfast is served in the restaurant, and there's a small bar.

Mena House Oberoi

Shari' Al Ahram (near the Giza Pyramids); tel: 02-3377 3222; www.menahouseoberoi.com; ££££

Built in 1869 as Khedive Ismail's hunting lodge, the Mena House is an historic landmark and a Cairene institution. Its guest list reads like a Who's

Who of world history and includes Churchill, General Montgomery and Jimmy Carter. The rooms in the old wing are highly atmospheric and beautifully decorated with antiques and modern art; some have heart-stopping views of the pyramids; the less expensive garden-annexe is also comfortable, and some rooms have pyramid views. There's also a large pool, a golf course, several restaurants with excellent reputations, various bars and a nightclub.

Osiris

12th floor, 49 Shari' Nubar, Bab Al Louq, Downtown; tel: 02-2794 5728; http://hotelosiris.free.fr; £

The Osiris is run by a French-Egyptian couple and their family and remains a firm favourite among travellers for its homely, intimate vibe. The location (the top floor of a concrete building) may not look promising, but inside it's bright, immaculate and simply but tastefully furnished. There's also a pleasant rooftop terrace with views across Cairo.

Pension Roma

169 Shari' Muhammad Farid, Downtown; tel: 02-2391 1088; £

A long-time favourite of frequent visitors to Cairo, the French-Egyptian Madame Cressaty keeps her pension with pride. Rooms of the 1940s-style Roma boast tall ceilings, old wooden floors and an airy, Old-World feel. Half-board is also available.

President Hotel

22 Shari' Dr Taha Hussein, Zamalik; tel: 02-2735 0718; email: preshotl@ thewayout.net; ££–£££

The rooms don't quite match the upmarket lobby, but the President's still a good-value mid-range option. Set in a quiet residential neighbourhood, it offers a business centre, friendly staff, a patisserie and a lively top-floor bar/restaurant serving decent *mezze*.

Le Riad

114 Shari' Al Mu'ez Li Dinillah, Islamic Cairo; tel: 02-2924 1147; email: leriad.cairo@yahoo.fr; ££££

Just five minutes' walk from Khan Al Khalili in Islamic Cairo, this boutique hotel enjoys a great location, spacious and sumptuous rooms (featuring plasma TVs and computers) and a lovely, large roof terrace-restaurant.

Talisman Boutique Hotel

5th floor, 39 Shari' Tal'at Harb, Downtown; tel: 02-2393 943; www.talisman-hotel-com; £££–££££

Cairo's first boutique has 24 spacious, stylish and individually decorated rooms. There's also an atmospheric breakfast room and various salons to relax in after the day's sightseeing. Owners and fervent Cairophiles Véronique and Yusuf love to share their passion for the city and can advise on guides and tours. Hard to find (look for the alleyway opposite the A l'Américaine coffee shop), but worth the hunt.

Above from far left: room in the modern garden annexe of the Mena House; drinks at the Sofitel Old Winter Palace, Luxor (see p.114).

Windsor

19 Shari' Al Alfi, Downtown; tel:
02-2591 5277; www.windsorcairo.
com; ££

For nostalgic souls keen to conjure up
a Cairo of bygone days, the Windsor
is the place. The old lift, worn marble
floors, sunken sofas and fading Moorish
decor hint at its former splendour.
Faded it may be, but it's a downtown
institution, and the atmospheric first-
floor bar remains a popular watering
hole for foreign correspondents.

Alexandria

Hotel Crillon

3rd floor, 5 Shari' Adib Ishaq;
tel: 03-480 0330; £

With a central location, lashings of
old-fashioned character, friendly and
attentive staff, spick-and-span rooms
at great prices (some with harbour
views), the Crillon is the best budget
bet in town.

Egypt Hotel

1 Degla, Shari' Abdel Hamid
Badawy (one block from Athineos
patisserie); tel: 03-481 4483; ££

Price for a standard double
room for one night, including
taxes and breakfast, during
peak season:

££££	over £65
£££	£25–65
££	£10–25
£	under £10

This centrally situated hotel offers
comfortable, spacious and well-furnished rooms and is efficiently run by
friendly and helpful staff. It takes the
mid-range crown in Alexandria. Ask
for a room with sea views.

Four Seasons Alexandria

Corniche, San Stefano; tel: 03-581
8080; www.fourseasons.com/
alexandria; ££££

Alexandria's newest and most sumptuous hotel offers capacious rooms
that are decked out with antiques
and digital mod-cons and have ocean
views. The service is lavish, and facilities include an infinity pool, private
beach and marina.

Sofitel Cecil Hotel

16 Meadan Saad Zaghloul; tel: 03-487
7173; www.sofitel.com; ££££

The Cecil's long been an Alexandrine
institution, with Noel Coward, Som-
erset Maugham and Lawrence Durrell
all having stayed here. The glamour
has long gone, but it remains an
atmospheric and romantic place with
good service. The comfortable rooms
boast sweeping bay views.

Windsor Palace Hotel

Shari' Ash-Shohada, Corniche; tel:
03-480 8123; www.paradiseinn
egypt.com; £££–££££

Another city institution, the grand
old Edwardian dame was sympatheti-
cally renovated in the late 1990s and

now combines impressive and original period glamour (including the lavish stucco ornamentation, grand lobby and period lifts) with modern comforts and luxuries.

Al Moudira

Daba'iyya, West Bank (12km/7½ miles south of the ticket office via Memnon Colossi); tel: 012-325 1307; www.moudira.com; £££–££££

Designed by the French-Egyptian architect Olivier Sednaoui, the Al Moudira looks like a Moorish palace-meets-hammam. Beautifully laid out around a central courtyard-garden, the huge rooms are individually and attentively furnished. There's also an extensive garden, a serene pool and a reputable restaurant *(see p.119)*, but it's the tranquillity and impeccable service that really make it stand out.

Amoun Al Gazila

Geziret Al Bairat, West Bank (near the ferry landing, left at the Mobil petrol station); tel: 095-231 0912; £

The building itself is nothing special, but it is the setting amid sugar-cane fields, the views over the Theban hills, delicious breakfasts in the verdant garden and the fantastic home cooking that make this delightful family-run place really special. Rooms are simple but clean, and rates depend on facilities (some have private bathrooms).

Beit Sabée

Near Madinat Habu Temple, Kom Lolah, West Bank; tel: 010-632 4926; email: info@nourelnil.com; ££

The Beit Sabée is a beguiling mud-brick house with simple but tasteful rooms done out in local palettes, textiles and furnishings. With just eight rooms, it's stylish but intimate and homely, and has even graced the pages of *Elle Decoration* magazine.

Marsam Hotel

Opposite Valley of the Nobles, West Bank; tel: 095-2372 403; www.luxor-westbank.com/marsam_e_az.htm; £

The West Bank's original hotel, built close to the major site of Luxor, the Marsam (formerly the Sheikh Ali Hotel) was built in the 1920s to house archaeologists. It still does. A delightful domed mud-brick hotel, it offers 30 very simple but clean and tranquil rooms situated around a courtyard, with good home cooking to boot.

New Emilio Hotel

Shari' Yousef Hassan, East Bank; tel: 095-237 3570; emilio_hotel@ hotmail.com; ££

Ever-popular for its comfortable rooms equipped with satellite TV, fridge, telephone and air-con, as well as a business centre, sauna, small pool and sun deck on the roof, the Emilio represents Luxor's best mid-range option.

Above from far left: the Windsor, in Cairo; the grand entrance to the Sofitel Old Winter Palace, Luxor *(see p.114)*; the Four Seasons Alexandria.

Philippe Hotel

Shari' Dr Labib Habashy, East Bank; tel: 095-238 0050; fax: 095-238 0050; £££

The Philippe offers spotless air-conditioned rooms with television and fridge, some with balconies, plus roof terrace, small pool and bar, which makes it a long-standing favourite with tour groups. Book well ahead.

Sofitel Old Winter Palace

Corniche An Nil, East Bank; tel: 095-238 0425; ££££

One of Egypt's most historic hotels, this is a national institution. Built in 1886 to house Europe's young aristocrats doing their Grand Tours, this hotel has hosted all of Luxor's visiting notables from Tsar Nicholas II and Agatha Christie to Howard Carter and Lady Diana. Victorian-palatial in design, it also boasts acres of luscious formal gardens, a gorgeous pool, tennis courts and some first-class restaurants. Rooms are spacious and comfortable; many have unbeatable views over the Nile. Historic and romantic, comfortable and well run, it's worth a splurge.

> Price for a standard double room for one night, including taxes and breakfast, during peak season:
>
> | | |
> |---|---|
> | ££££ | over £65 |
> | £££ | £25–65 |
> | ££ | £10–25 |
> | £ | under £10 |

Sonesta St George Hotel

Shari' Khaled Ibn Al Walid, East Bank; tel: 095-238 2575; www.sonesta.com/egypt_Luxor; £££–££££

It's not the most handsome building in town, but the well-managed St George offers some of the best amenities and rooms at some of the best prices. Rooms are well furnished, comfortable and spacious (some have direct views over the Nile), and there's a large pool with sun deck and sunken bar, several outdoor jacuzzis, a gym and a couple of good restaurants *(see p.120)*.

Beyt el-Kerem

North of the Tombs of the Nobles, West Bank; tel: 019-2399 443 (Holland tel: +31-6-8118 0400); www.experiencenubia.com; £

Run by a Nubian and Dutch couple, this modern house has an attractive roof terrace, lovely views and good home cooking. Rooms (with shared bathroom) are very simple but clean, and the hotel is welcoming and peaceful. A good range of activities, including fishing, painting and Nile swimming, can be organised. To get here, take the ferry opposite the railway station to the West Bank. It's then a five-minute walk north along the river.

Isis Hotel

Corniche An Nil, East Bank; tel: 097-231 7400; www.pyramisaegypt.com; £££

The Isis has comfortable chalet-style rooms set in a garden with a pool and a couple of restaurants serving European cuisine. It is also centrally located right next to the Nile.

Keylany Hotel

25 Shari' Keylany, East Bank; tel: 097-232 3134; www.keylanyhotel.com; ££
Offering simple but clean and well-furnished rooms with air-conditioning, satellite television and private bathrooms, the Keylany is Aswan's best budget bet. The management is efficient and helpful, and there's a pleasant roof terrace for drinks, a small pool and spa, plus an in-house internet café.

Mövenpick Resort Aswan

Elephantine Island; tel: 097-230 3455; www.moevenpick-aswan.com; ££££
Despite an unattractive exterior (with air traffic control-style tower), this is one of Aswan's best places to stay. Recently renovated, the luxury spa hotel occupies the northern tip of the island and has its own ferry service. Facilities include a garden, pool and good spa facilities.

Sofitel Old Cataract Hotel

Shari' Abtal At Tahrir; tel: 097-231 6000; www.sofitel.com; ££££
Set on a rock about the river, this is, according to many, the Nile's most iconic and historic hotel. Agatha Christie, one in a gallery of VIP guests, is said to have part-written *Death on the Nile* here (it also served as the set of

the movie). Due to open in May 2011, this Moorish-meets-modern hotel will comprise only deluxe suites, a vast terrace, a huge spa area and a spectacular wellness centre. *See also p.120.*

Abu Simbel

Eskaleh

Tel: 012-368 0521; email: fikrykachif@genevalink.com; ££
The Beit An Nubi ('Nubian place'), a delightful mud-brick hotel-cum-cultural centre, is owned by Nubian musician Fikry Kachif. The five rooms are simple but comfortable with immaculate private bathrooms; some have their own terrace overlooking the lake. There's also a library with books about all aspects of Nubian culture, a roof terrace where musicians sometimes play, and a good restaurant that uses ingredients from the organic garden.

Nefertari Hotel

Tel: 097-340 0510; £££
The Nefertari might have basic, uninspiring rooms (and management), but it is located close to the temple, and its swimming pool overlooks the lake.

Seti Abu Simbel

On Lake Nasser; tel: 097-340 0720; www.setifirst.com; ££££
Abu Simbel's only five-star hotel has chalet-style rooms set in a garden fronting Lake Nasser. Comfortable, well equipped and tranquil, though a little overpriced.

Above from far left: interior and riverside view of the Sofitel Old Cataract Hotel, Aswan; the Sofitel Cecil Hotel, Alexandria (see p.112).

For millennia, it has catered to travellers, ambassadors and conquerors; today the Nile Valley is still the source of some of Egypt's best food. With fish from the river, abundant fruit and vegetables from the fields either side, and hoards of hungry, well-heeled tourists seeking sustenance, the Nile provides fertile ground for decent dining.

Cosmopolitan Cairo offers everything from *koshari* stands to five-star all-you-can-eat buffets and menus designed by top international chefs. Alexandria is most famous for fish and seafood; Luxor and Aswan, though more limited in choice, often offer better value for money.

Essentially, there's a choice between three types of eating establishment: the large, licensed hotel-restaurants; the plush Middle Eastern or international-themed tourist establishments; and the small, street-side independents. Head to the first two for fine dining and alcohol, to the last for culinary authenticity and astonishing value.

The dress code for all but the basic places is smart/casual. Booking is advised at the weekends in the more expensive places. *See also Food and Drink p.14–17, and the blue food and drink boxes throughout the Walks and Tours chapter.*

Cairo

Abou as-Sid

157 Shari' 26 July, Zamalek; tel: 02-2735-9640; daily noon–midnight; ££–£££

Funky boudoir-cum-orientalist fantasy, this is currently one of Cairo's restaurant hotspots. Intimate and colourful, it has a strong local flavour: the walls are adorned with local artwork, it plays modern Egyptian beats and serves traditional Egyptian food and drink, including local versions of classic cocktails. Atmospheric and fun, it invites settling in. If you fancy trying a *sheesha*, here's the place to do it.

Akher Sa'a

8 Shari' Al Alfy, Downtown; tel: 02-2575 1668; 24hrs; £

With a fervent local following, Akher Sa'a is known to serve some of the best *fuul* and *ta'amiyya* sandwiches in town spiced up with great sauces and 'extras' including *soyuk* (spicy sausage). The food's fresh and well made, and the prices are rock-bottom. The sign (and menu) is only in Arabic; look for queues at the takeaway section, with a simple sitting area next door.

The Bird Cage

Semiramis InterContinental, Corniche An Nil, Garden City; tel: 02-2795 7171; daily noon–midnight; ££–£££

When you've had your fill of *mezze* dishes or crave a culinary break, head for the Bird Cage. It's known for its well-prepared, well-presented Thai food served in tranquil and discreet surrounds. Try the speciality: sea bass steamed in banana leaves, or the deep-fried prawns in *konafa* (angel hair).

Centro Recreativo Italiano

40 Shari' 26 July, Bulak; tel: 02-2575 9590; daily 9am–11pm; ££

Designed for Italians by Italians, the Centro serves as the Italian Social Club and is *the* place to come for authentic Italian pizzas. There's a cover charge of LE10 to non-members, but prices for both food and (Italian) wine are reasonable. In summer, dining's alfresco in the compound.

Citadel View Restaurant

Al Azhar Park, Shari' Salah Salem; tel: 02-2510 9151; www.alazhar park.com; daily noon–midnight; £££

Aptly named, the Citadel View is a pseudo-Fatimid palace that boasts gorgeous views over the Al Azhar's formal gardens, the Citadel and Old Cairo from the restaurant terraces and café. Food is French-influenced but specialises in typical with Egyptian-style grilled meat fests. At weekends, there's a popular open buffet (LE130). Lantern-lit and intimate it's a good place for dinner *à deux*, or during the day, a cool and tranquil lunch.

Fish Market

Americana boat, 26 Shari' An Nil, Giza; tel: 02-3570 9693; daily noon–midnight; ££

Occupying the upper deck of a boat permanently moored on the Nile is the aptly named Fish Market. Choose from the daily catch, or ask the *maître d'* for recommendations, then watch as it's weighed and carefully cooked. With excellent and reasonably priced *mezze* and salads to boot, a unique atmosphere and lovely views across the river, it makes for an agreable evening.

Koshari et-Tahrir

Shari' At Tahrir, near Meadan At Tahrir; daily 8am–midnight: £

This restaurant is considered by many Cairenes to be *the* place to come for Egypt's famous, quasi-national dish, *koshari*. Busy and buzzy, it's worth the wait, queues and crowds particularly at weekends.

Sequoia

3 Shari' Abu Al Feda, Zamalik; tel: 02-2576 8086; daily noon–midnight; ££–£££

Located by the water on the northern tip of the island is the popular Sequoia. With its informal and laid-back atmosphere, consistent and reasonably priced food, swift service and mellow music, plus the largest selection of waterpipes in Cairo, it's hugely popular. Reservations are essential, particularly at the weekend.

Above from far left: Cairo's Citadel View Restaurant and Sequoia.

Price for a two-course meal for one person, including a glass of wine.

££££	over £50
£££	£25–50
££	£5–25
£	under £5

Alexandria

Abu Ashraf

28 Shari' Safar Pasha, Bahari; tel:
03-481 6597; daily 24hrs; £–££

Located in Alexandria's Anfushi
district (famous for its plethora of
street-side fish restaurants), is the
much-loved Abu Ashraf. Though
little more than tables under an
canopy, the fish and seafood is fresh
and expertly cooked. Point at the
fish you fancy, agree the price by its
weight, then request the way you want
it cooked. The fish casserole is also a
local favourite, particularly during the
winter months.

Centro de Portugal

42 Shari' Abd Al Kader, off Shari'
Kafr Abduh, Rushdy; tel: 03-542
7599; daily 6pm–1am; ££

If you're fed up with fish, the Por-
tuguese Social Club makes a good
culinary antidote, serving what many
European expats consider the best
steak au poivre and *frites* in town. It
also offers a good range of other
meat-based dishes as well as pasta and
ice-cold beer in an attractive garden.

Fish Market

Corniche An Nil, Bahari (near the
Kashafa Club); tel: 03-480 5119;
daily noon–midnight; ££–£££

Ranking among Alexandria's best fish
restaurants, the restaurant boasts beautiful views over the harbour, upmarket
decor and service, and an impressive

daily catch laid out on ice. Though
increasingly popular with tour groups,
the food and service remains consistently good.

Mohammed Ahmed

17 Shari' Shakor Pasha, near
Meadan Ramla; tel: 03-487 3576;
daily 6am–midnight; £

Much loved locally for its *fuul* and
ta'amiyya sandwiches served with a
variety of sauces and condiments, as
well as *fiteer* and other Egyptian
savouries, Mohammed Ahmed offers
both takeaway and eat-in options.
Menus are in English and Arabic, and
it's a great choice for vegetarians.

Samakmak

42 Qasr Ras At Tin (near the Citadel
of Qayetbay); tel: 03-481 1560; daily
10am–midnight; ££

Owned by an Alexandrine former
belly dancer, this restaurant is best
known for its range of fish and seafood (including calamari, clams and
crab) and for its imaginative way of
preparing them. Cosy and intimate,
it also serves delicious bread, *mezze*,
salads and rice accompaniments.

Trianon

Corner of Saad Zaghloul and
Meadan Ramla; tel: 03-482 0986;
daily 7am–midnight; £–££

One of Alexandria's culinary institutions, the Trianon has wooden
panelling, intricate decoration and an

Old-World feel. The lovingly restored restaurant serves Mediterranean-meets-Levantine meat and vegetarian dishes, while next door, there's a popular patisserie with a terrace – perfect for Alexandrine-watching over a hearty breakfast (try the omelettes) or a reviving cup of tea and a cake.

Luxor

1886

Winter Palace Hotel, Corniche An Nil, East Bank; tel: 012-238 0422; daily 7pm–midnight; ££££

The Winter Palace's flagship restaurant, 1886 has long reigned as Luxor's top table. Keen not to let its standards drop, the restaurant has a dress code of jacket and tie, and the service in the rarefied dining room is formal and attentive. French-style with Egyptian influence and ingredients, the cuisine is creative and sumptuous, though the mark-up on the wine list is very steep.

African Garden Restaurant

Al Gezira, West Bank; tel: 012-365 8722; daily 10am–11pm; £–££

> Price for a two-course meal for one person, including a glass of wine.
>
> | | |
> |---|---|
> | ££££ | over £50 |
> | £££ | £25–50 |
> | ££ | £5–25 |
> | £ | under £5 |

Located around 100m/yds straight up from the ferry terminal, the African's biggest plus is its large, verdant and shaded terrace. Prices have increased recently, and the food's good but not outstanding, but the three-course local-style lunch and dinner for LE30 is good value. Pizzas, pasta, soups and salads also feature on the menu.

Al Moudira

Al Moudira Hotel, Daba'iyya, West Bank (10km/6 miles south of the Valley of the Queens); tel: 012-325 1307; daily 7am–10.30pm; ££–£££

With seating either inside the Moorish-inspired hotel, or around an ornamental pool in the delightful courtyard-garden, the Moudira offers imaginative, well-presented and beautifully cooked European-Middle Eastern fusion cooking. The service is impeccable, and the atmosphere intimate, romantic and tranquil. It's the perfect place for dinner *à deux*.

Bombay Restaurant

Shari' Khaled Ibn Al Walid, East Bank (near the Sheraton Hotel); tel: 012-238 7935; daily noon–midnight; ££

For those keen for a night off from kebabs and *kofta*, the Bombay Restaurant might just fit the bill. It offers a decent selection of classic curries with all the usual trimmings including naan breads, poppadoms and samosas. It's a great choice for vegetarians, and prices are reasonable.

Above from far left: typical *mezze* dishes; sweet treats for sale on Alexandria's Corniche.

In general, mid- and
upper-range restau-
rants serve alcohol
(including beer and
wine), as do a few
lower-range eateries,
if they cater regularly
to tourists.

Koshary El-Zaeem

Meadan Hussain, East Bank;
daily 24hrs; £

With a fervent local following,
Koshary El-Zaeem is considered one
of Aswan's best *koshari* joints. Hearty
portions are topped with generous
amounts of spicy tomato sauce and
fried onion. Most people opt for
takeaway food, but you can sit and eat
at one of the dusty tables, if you can
find one that's free.

Miyako Restaurant

Sonesta St George Hotel, Shari'
Khaled Ibn Al Walid, East Bank; tel:
012-238 2575; daily noon–11pm; £££

Popular in particular for its *teppanyaki*
prepared by chefs in front of you, the
Miyako also offers reasonable sushi,
sashimi and saki. Cool, low-lit and
peaceful, it makes a pleasant tempo-
rary retreat from the street heat, dust
and din.

Snobs

Off Shari' Khaled Ibn Al Walid, East
Bank (near Sonesta Hotel); tel: 012-
236 0356; daily noon–midnight; £–££

Snobs restaurant serves fresh, well-
cooked and slightly more imaginative
Western fare than is the average in
Egypt. Pizza, pasta, salads, soups and
steaks are home-made and reasonably
priced. Representing good value, it's
also well managed and friendly.

Tutankhamun

200m/yds south of the ferry landing;
West Bank; tel: 012-231 0918; daily
noon–11pm; £

This simple, rustic Egyptian restaurant's biggest asset is its cooling
and relaxed roof terrace, which
affords fantastic views over the Nile.
Mahmoud, the charming *patron*, is
renowned for his home-made *tagens*
(casseroles cooked in covered clay
pots baked in the oven). His 'rose-
mary chicken' served with sweet
oriental rice is famous.

Aswan

1902 Restaurant

Old Cataract Hotel, Shari' Abtal At
Tahrir; East Bank; tel: 097-231 6000;
daily noon–11pm; £££–££££

The Old Cataract's pride and joy, and
the top restaurant in town, 1902 is currently undergoing like the hotel itself
(see p.115), a major facelift. When
it reopens (billed for May 2011), it
should reintroduce its fine formula
of French-meets-Levantine cuisine
served up in the grand dining room.
European wines are available, but the
mark-up's astronomical.

Price for a two-course meal
for one person, including a
glass of wine.

££££	over £50
£££	£25–50
££	£5–25
£	under £5

Al Masry

Shari' Al Matar; East Bank; tel: 097-230 2576; daily noon–midnight; £

The decor might be slightly orientalist-kitsch, but the little Al Masry claims to do the best kebabs and *kofta* in town, along with succulent and tasty chicken and sometimes pigeon and quail. Sold by weight or size, cooked to perfection and served in large portions with lashings of tahini, *khobz* (bread) and salad, it's a great place to come for fresh, first-rate local food at unbeatable prices.

Aswan Moon

Corniche An Nil, East Bank; tel: 097-231 6108; daily 11am–midnight; £–££

The town's most famous floating restaurant, the Aswan Moon boasts a great setting, friendly service and a lively atmosphere. In the high season, entertainment is usually staged nightly. The food (traditional Levantine favourites such as kebabs and roast chicken) is variable, but it's really the ambience that you come for.

Koshary Ali Baba Restaurant

Shari' Abtal At Tahrir, East Bank; no tel; daily 10am–midnight; £

It may not look much, but Ali Baba is considered the town's top *koshari* joint. Simple and clean, serving excellent *koshari* cooked daily, it's a great place to come to try Egypt's famous, carb-heavy dish, though prices do tend to rise for tourists.

Panorama

Corniche An Nil, East Bank; tel: 097-231 6169; daily 10am–midnight; £

Situated opposite the Hanafi Souq, the Panorama is well named, with a pleasant and cool terrace overlooking the river. With its menu of fresh fruit and herb juices (including *karkadeh* – hibiscus) and simple but delicious meat and vegetable dishes (*mezzes* and mains), it's a great place to come for honest Egyptian home cooking.

Above from far left: Aswan's 1902 restaurant; a wonderful array of spices is used in Egyptian cooking.

Below: *mezze*, a light, fresh meal.

NIGHTLIFE

The towns and cities along the Nile may not be known for their nightlife, but it's still worth seeking out. Usually colourful, culturally insightful and lots of fun, it runs the gamut from seedy belly-dancing bars, to Sufi Whirling Dervish shows and late-night café culture. *See also p.22–3.*

See also p.22–3.

Dance

The more upmarket belly-dancing shows can be pricey but usually include a meal (though not drinks). Shows officially start at midnight, though performers often do not take the stage until 1 or 2am. Examples include the Casablanca Club (Sheraton Hotel, Meadan Al Galaa; tel: 02-3336 9700; charge).

Cheaper, less predictable and usually more fun (particularly if you want to join in) are the clubs in downtown Cairo, such as on Shari' Alfy, though some venues verge on the seedy. Two tolerable examples are Scheherazade (Shari' Alfy, Downtown; tel: 02-2658 5287; charge) and Palmyra (off Shari' 26 July, Downtown; tel: 02-3561 8716; charge).

Sufi Dancing

Some of the top-end hotels and cruise ships also put on Sufi-style shows complete with whirling dervishes, musicians and singers.

In Cairo, the excellent Wikala Al Ghuri (150m/yds southeast of pedestrian bridge off Shari' Al Azhar; tel: 02-2512 1735; free) hosts a nightly performance by the colourful and energetic Al Tannoura Egyptian Heritage Dance Troupe; get there an hour early to guarantee a seat.

Music

Cairo has a plethora of places to hear a wide mix of music. Apart from the clubs listed separately below, other good ones include: El Sawy Culture Wheel (Shari' 26 July, Zamalik; tel: 02-2736 8881; www.culturewheel.com; daily 9am–9pm; charge); El Genaina Theatre (Shari' Salah Salem, Al Azhar Park; tel: 02-2362 6748; www.mawred.org; charge), and the Citadel (Shari' Salah Salem; tel: 02-2512 1735; usually free). They host touring bands from Egypt, the Middle East and the West.

After Eight

6 Shari' Qasr An Nil, Downtown; tel: 02-2574 0855; www.after8egypt. com; charge

Located down an alley, this spot is funky, atmospheric and eclectic, with music ranging from live jazz and salsa Egyptian DJs and foreign bands.

Cairo Jazz Club

197 Shari' 26 July, Agouza; tel: 02-3345 9939; www.cairojazzclub. com; daily 5pm–3am; charge

Cairo's only live jazz venue is packed nightly (reservations required via the website or telephone), and stages an eclectic mixture of Egyptian, Arab and Western-influenced music.

Makan

1 Shari' Saad Zaghloul, Mounira; tel: 02-2792 0878; www.egyptmusic. org; charge

The place to hear authentic traditional music, Makan hosts regular and eclectic live performances ranging from traditional local orchestras to meditation and healing rituals.

Nightlife

Cairo boasts Egypt's biggest quantity and quality of bars, ranging from the sleazy downtown dives to the trendy hotspots of Zamalik and Mohandessin, and the plush, cocktail-toting lounges of the five-star hotels. The street cafés (which don't serve alcohol) provide a insight into the city's nocturnal life.

Discos are found in all the Nile's towns (though they're confined to the larger hotels and restaurants outside Cairo). Most have a dress code and can refuse entry to single males (particularly in large groups). Dancing usually kicks off after 11pm.

As the clubbing scene is relatively small in Cairo, and venues come and go, you'll need to ask around. Check listings *(see margin, right)* for one-off events.

Bars in Cairo
L'Aubergine

1st floor, 5 Shari' Sayed Al Bakry, Zamalik; tel: 02-2735 6550

This trendy, minimalist bar is located in the heart of Zamalik and is popular with university (AUC) students.

Topkapi

Opposite the Four Seasons Hotel, Corniche An Nil, Garden City; charge

Little more than a tent and a terrace overlooking the Nile, Topkapi is known for its DJs spinning trendy tunes and for *sheeshas* and *mezze*.

Windsor Hotel Bar

19 Shari' Alfi Bey, Downtown; tel: 02-2591 5277

Something of a Cairo institution, this colonial relic has cultivated a reputation for whimsical waiters serving a variety of beers.

Nightclubs in Cairo
Absolute

Casino Es Shagara, Corniche An Nil, Bulaq; tel: 02-2579 6511; charge

Absolute is where Cairo's well-heeled young things go at weekends. It has a great location on the river, large dance floor and good DJs.

Africana

Shari' Al Haram, Giza; charge

This club plays disco music from all across the African continent.

Latex

Nile Hilton; 1113 Corniche An Nil, Downtown; tel: 02-2578 0444; charge

Latex continues to draw in the 20-somethings with its house-mix.

Above from far left: locals and tourist hit the streets of Alexandria by night; Cairo is the best place along the Nile to go clubbing.

Listings
Events and entertainment listings can be found in the daily *Egyptian Gazette*, the weekly *Al Ahram*, *Croc*, the *Egyptian Mail on Saturday* and *Cairo Magazine*, as well as the monthly *Egypt Today*. You can also check out the websites: www.yallabina. com and www. omeldonia.com.

Film
Arabic films are rarely subtitled, but around half a dozen cinemas in Cairo screen English films with or without Arabic subtitles; check the listings sections of the papers and magazines *(see above)* for more details.

GLOSSARY

'ahwa	Egyptian coffee house or coffee
ankh	hieroglyphic sign for life resembling a looped cross
Apis	sacred bull of Memphis
bab	gate, door
baksheesh	tip, gratuity
canopic jars	containers used for storing organs of deceased in tombs
caravanserai	merchant's inn or lodge
cartouche	oval-shaped, hieroglyphic 'label' bearing the pharaoh or god's name
corniche	road along a bank of the Nile
hammam	traditional bathhouse
hypostyle	a chamber with a ceiling supported by columns
khan	see *caravanserai*
khanqah	Sufi community residence
khedive	Egyptian viceroy during time of Ottomans
kuttub	Quranic school (lit: 'books')
madrasah	school (often attached to a mosque)
mashrabiyya	intricately carved wooden screen or panel
mastaba	mudbrick, bench-shaped structure above tombs (lit: 'bench')
midan	town square
mihrab	niche in a mosque that indicates Mecca's direction
moulid	the birthday of a saint or holy man
muqarna	stalactite-like stone carving used in Islamic decoration
pronaos	porch with columns leading to naos (enclosed 'Holy of Holies' in a temple)
pylon	monumental gateway to a temple preceding a court
qasr	fort or castle
sabil	public drinking fountain
sabil kuttab	type of non-congregational mosque found in Cairo
shari'	road, street
sheesha	water pipe used for smoking
souq	bazaar, market

AUTHOR'S THANKS

Publishing space restrictions sadly make it impossible to thank the countless individuals who showed me the famous Egyptian warmth, kindness, and eagerness to please, and I can only single out: Amgad Barakat, Ghada Salah, Ahmed Younis, Mona Halim, Hassan Hossam, Nasr Hashem of Mövenpick; Mohamed El Abhar and the Carlton Hotel, Cairo; Abdul and all staff at Beit El-Kerem, Aswan; Madame Zeina and Konny Mathews at Al Moudira, Luxor; Gemma Frenzel, Linda Petrie, Olivia Warburton, Erin O'Connor, and Richard Launay of Sofitel; Samir Azer, Sonesta St George; Tarek Lotfy of Mena House, Cairo; Mahmoud Abd Al Mola, guide. Special thanks to: Khaled Ramy, Director of Egypt's Tourism Board, London, and Rasha Azaizi, Deputy Director; and above all, Mr Wagdy Soliman, Manager of Soliman Travel and all his staff in Cairo; Professor Fekri Hassan, Cairo; Mr Habib Aidroos, EgyptAir Sales Manager UK & Ireland; and Professor Dr Zahi Hawass, Secretary General, Supreme Council of Antiquities, all of whom so generously gave up so much of their time to contribute to this book. Big thanks, finally, to Insight's Alex Knights, Zoë Goodwin, James Macdonald, Naomi Peck and, especially, Siân Lezard and Clare Peel, two outstanding editors. I dedicate this book to Billie Skrine, an extraordinary woman.

CREDITS

Insight Step by Step The Nile

Written by: Frances Linzee Gordon and Sylvie Franquet

Series Editor: Clare Peel

Editors: Siân Lezard and Naomi Peck

Map Production: APA Cartography Department

Picture Manager: Steven Lawrence

Art Editors: Ian Spick and Richard Cooke

Photography: **All Pictures** APA Glyn Genin except: AKG London 32T; Ahmed Al Badawy 48–9, 55T; P Ankur 7TL, 24–5; Gaynor Barton 112TL; Bastique 64T; Vinicius Batista 56T, 116T; Michael Brannon 70T; Vincent Brown 24TL; Neil Carey 80M; David Corcoran 4MT; Neil Cummings 98BL; David Dennis 8TL, 98BM; David Evers 40T, 44–5, 122T; Andrew Griffith 8BM, 18B; Son Of Groucho 88B; Freeparking 62T; Francis Frith 33T; Furibond 54M; David Haberthur 31T; Matt Hampson 79; Allan Harries 22–3; Tom Hartley 79M; ENIT/Hemis 2–3, 2BM/BR, 8–9, 8MM, 12M, 28T, 34–5, 68T, 74T, 84T, 91T, 97TR, 114–15, 114TL; iStock-photo 26TL, 27TR, 80T; Tim Kelly 4MB, 7BR, 46–7; Gary Ku 53M; Leonardo 121T; Ricardo Liberato 23TR; Ian McKellar 8BL; madmedea 64MT; Meryan 25TR; Dan Nevill 49TR; Bob Partridge 8ML, 11TR, 26–7, 34BM; Guillen Perez 102–3; Photolibrary 7TR, 12–13, 17T, 37T, 38–9, 38TL, 48BR, 57, 58TL, 59TL, 63TR, 79B, 82BR; J Pinkney 2BL, 101T; Jeffrey Riman 18T; Risastia 39TR; Keith Schengili-Roberts 98MR; Simon Po 117T; Divya Thakur 6B, 14–15; Maurice Thaler 8MR; John Thomas 7MR, 22TL; Tips Images 72BR, 120T, 123Micahel Tyler 113TR; Upyernoz 62–3; Ed Yourdon 7BL, 12B, 16T, 20B, 88M, 89T, 102TL, 106T. **Front cover**: main image: Photolibrary; bottom left: iStockphoto; bottom right: iStockphoto. Flap images: images reused from interior of book, credits as above; other images: iStockphoto.

Printed by: CTPS-China

CONTACTING THE EDITORS

We would appreciate it if readers would alert us to errors or outdated information by writing to us at insight@apaguide.co.uk or APA Publications, PO Box 7910, London SE1 1WE, UK.

DISTRIBUTION

Worldwide

APA Publications GmbH & Co. Verlag KG (Singapore branch)

7030 Ang Mo Kio Ave 5, 08-65 Northstar @ AMK Singapore 569880. Email: apasin@singnet.com.sg

UK and Ireland

GeoCenter International Ltd

Meridian House, Churchill Way West, Basingstoke, Hampshire, RG21 6YR.

Email: sales@geocenter.co.uk

US

Ingram Publisher Services

One Ingram Blvd, PO Box 3006, La Vergne, TN 37086-1986.

Email: customer.service@ingrampublisherservices.com

Australia

Universal Publishers

1 Waterloo Road, Macquarie Park, NSW 2113.

Email: sales@universalpublishers.com.au

New Zealand

Hema Maps New Zealand Ltd (HNZ)

Unit 2, 10 Cryers Road, East Tamaki, Auckland 2013.

Email: sales.hema@clear.net.nz

www.insightguides.com

INDEX